CRICUT
for Beginners

The Ultimate Guide for beginners to INSTANTLY MASTER CRICUT WITH SECRET TIPS AND HACKS!

Hope Ziegler Rojas

Text Copyright © [Hope Ziegler Rojas]

All rights reserved. No part of this guide may be reproduced in any form without permission in writing from the publisher except in the case of brief quotations embodied in critical articles or reviews.

Legal & Disclaimer

The information contained in this book and its contents is not designed to replace or take the place of any form of medical or professional advice; and is not meant to replace the need for independent medical, financial, legal or other professional advice or services, as may be required. The content and information in this book has been provided for educational and entertainment purposes only.

The content and information contained in this book has been compiled from sources deemed reliable, and it is accurate to the best of the Author's knowledge, information and belief. However, the Author cannot guarantee its accuracy and validity and cannot be held liable for any errors and/or omissions. Further, changes are periodically made to this book as and when needed. Where appropriate and/or necessary, you must consult a professional (including but not limited to your doctor, attorney, financial advisor or such other professional advisor) before using any of the suggested remedies, techniques, or information in this book.

Upon using the contents and information contained in this book, you agree to hold harmless the Author from and against any damages, costs, and expenses, including any legal fees potentially resulting from the application of any of the information provided by this book. This disclaimer applies to any loss, damages or injury caused by the use and application, whether directly or indirectly, of any advice or information presented, whether for breach of contract, tort, negligence, personal injury, criminal intent, or under any other cause of action.

You agree to accept all risks of using the information presented inside this book.

You agree that by continuing to read this book, where appropriate and/or necessary, you shall consult a professional (including but not limited to your doctor, attorney, or financial advisor or such other advisor as needed) before using any of the suggested remedies, techniques, or information in this book.

CRICUT MACHINES 7

USEFUL TERMINOLOGY 10

TOOLS & ACCESSORIES FOR YOUR CRICUT 18

MAKING STENCILS WITH CRICUT MACHINE 25

MAKING AN ENGRAVED GIFT TAG USING CRICUT MACHINE 27

MAKING STICKERS WITH CRICUT MACHINE 30

CUTTING SHRINK PLASTIC WITH A CRICUT MACHINE TO MAKE PHOTO ORNAMENTS 34

MAKING A BIRTHDAY CARD WITH CRICUT MACHINE 44

MAKING EARRINGS WITH CRICUT 51

THE CRICUT MAKER 3 55

SETTING UP YOUR CRICUT MACHINE 59

CRICUT MAKER 3 TOOLS AND ACCESSORIES NEEDED 65

HOW TO DESIGN ON CRICUT MAKER 3 84

VINYL FOR CRICUT PROJECTS 93

STEP BY STEP CRICUT PROJECTS TO GET STARTED 97

DOUBLE-SIDED TABLE RUNNER 97

SIMPLE DOOR DECAL PROJECT 109

PANTRY LABELS 125

CUSTOM PILLOWCASE   130

FREQUENTLY ASKED QUESTIONS ON CRICUT MAKER 3   136

CONCLUSION   139

Cricut Machines

The EasyPress 2

The EasyPress 2 isn't necessarily a Cricut cutting machine, but rather a heat-transfer machine that's specifically designed to assist with iron-on vinyls and other decals. Once you've used your Cricut machine to cut your design (with a heat transfer material, such as iron-on), you can then use the EasyPress 2 to help you adhere the design to the designated project surface.

The price of the EasyPress 2 machine is around $189 for the 9x9" and $239 for the 12x12". You can choose between the color options of raspberry, lilac, or mint. The 9x9" is a great option for medium projects such as t-shirts, pillowcases, etc., while the 12x12" option is great for larger projects such as hoodies, blankets, banners, etc. There is also an EasyPress Mini that's going for $69 if you generally want to handle much smaller iron-on designs.

There are also bundle options available when purchasing an EasyPress 2—for $109 you can get an EasyPress Mini with a starter Iron-On kit included, or a 9x9" EasyPress 2 with the starter Iron-On Kit for $209, or the 12x10" EasyPress 2 with the starter Iron-On kit for $259. The starter Iron-On kit has a few colors of iron-on sheets and a weeding toolset (which is used to weed away excess vinyl once the design has been cut). The starter Iron-On bundles are great for if you're starting off and would like to grab a few of the basic tools as well as a selection of iron-ons without paying for each one individually.

Alternatively, Cricut also offers the Everything Iron-On Bundle, which includes the weeding toolset, the essential toolset, and a few Iron-On vinyls along with a few funky colors. The bundle also comes with materials for you to practice with, along with the EasyPress Mini, all for $251,89. There are a few other bundle options such as the Basic Iron-On bundle, but there are various kits that come and go with the seasons.

The Cricut site currently only stocks the most recent machines such as the Maker, Explore Air 2, Joy, and the EasyPress machines. If you are looking for an older model, you may have to hunt down a second-hand one from someone who's selling (and you may be able to grab it at a bargain, and can also work in your favor in regard to learning on a cheaper and older model before stepping up to buy a newer, modern model).

The Cricut Maker

The Cricut Maker comes in color options of turquoise blue, lilac, mint, rose or champagne, and is currently priced at around $369. The site also offers bundles where you can grab an Essentials Bundle or an Everything Materials Bundle which includes different varieties of vinyls, pens, mats, and tool kits. The Essentials Bundle goes for around $533.42 while the Everything Bundle goes for around $637.83. However, Cricut was doing a special recently where the Essentials Bundle dropped to an amazing deal of $389.99 and the Everything Bundle was priced just $10 more, at $399.99, so it's worth finding out when Cricut has their holiday sales, clearance sales or promotions, as you can grab a brand new Maker *and* tool kits, mats, pens, and vinyls for around $200 less than the selling price on their site!

The Cricut Explore Air 2

The Explore Air 2 range also comes in a variety of colors that gorgeously wrap fully around the body of the machine. The color options are blue, mint, lilac, rose, and a neat-looking black. The model is priced at $249.99 and there are also bundle options available such as the Everything Bundle and the Essentials Bundle. The Everything Bundle is going for $487.83 and the Essentials Bundle is going for $383.42.

Lastly, the cute little Joy is priced at $179.99 (which is a much more affordable yet powerful option if you're looking to just specifically dabble with smaller projects such as cards, labels, and small designs). The Joy only comes in a standard blue and white color, and there are a few bundle options available such as the Label Making Bundle, Insert Card Bundle, Smart Vinyl Bundle, Smart Iron-On Bundle, and Essentials Bundle. The bundles vary around the price ranges of $235-$255. Similar to the Maker that has exclusive pens and blades for the machine, the Joy has a few vinyls (known as Smart Iron-Ons) that are created to work seamlessly with the Joy, if you're looking to add vinyl labels or designs to projects.

The Cricut Joy

On the Cricut website, you can also explore the range of tools and materials for the machines on their website, and the tools are categorized into different sections that pertain to the different Cricut models so that you know which tools work with which machines.

Useful Terminology

Cricut Design Space & Cricut Access

First and foremost, the "Cricut Design Space" is one of the tools which you will be using the most. Cricut Design Space is essentially a software that works off of a cloud which essentially acts as a bridge from your templates or whatever you'd like to cut or print, to your Cricut machine and gives it commands on how to go about cutting or printing pieces for your project (Microsoftsurfacedeals, 2016).

The Design Space also works with Cricut Access which is a library of images, designs, templates, patterns, and fonts for texts and quotes so that you can choose and import those that you'd like to incorporate into your project, into the 'canvas' on your design space. The canvas is essentially the main page in Design Space where you will create and alter the final design for your Cricut machine to cut or print. When you import images, etc. from Cricut Access, you'll then adjust it in your canvas so that it fits the measurements of your project surface, and then command your Cricut to start cutting or printing.

Mirror, Weld & Attach

Another important factor to consider when you're in Design Space and about to set up your Cricut machine to cut your design is that you'll need to 'mirror' your designs, especially if they include text. Mirroring is a function in Design Space and it essentially flips your design around so that it's cut the correct way. Most of your HTV projects will require you to mirror your design. If you have shiny HTV, you'll also need to remember to place the shiny side of the vinyl face-down when loading it into the machine.

If you'd like to save on as much material as possible and waste as little as possible, then you can also weld your design on Design Space. In doing so, you're moving the images, letters, or designs as close together as possible so that they touch and are then cut as one big piece rather than individually. If you weld your design, you're not only saving more material but you're also saving the time it takes to cut each piece individually and possibly also having to load the machine multiple times. Welding (meaning 'grouping' items together) needs to be done prior to your pressing cut, and once the design has been cut, you cannot undo the welding if you've saved it as is. If you'd like to keep your images and designs separate for later use, un-weld the items in Design Space after you've cut them, then save the project.

Similar to the Weld function, 'Attach' is another function in Design Space that allows you to keep the images and fonts as they are on the mat when you're cutting.

SVG Files

Scalable Vector Graphics are also known as 'SVG' files and are one of the most common file types to use for creating Cricut designs. You can import or export SVG files from Inkscape. SVG files don't rely on pixels, but rather 'vector' data to allow you to see the image (Morris, 2020). The fantastic thing about SVGs is that you can scale them to any resolution without compromising the quality of the 'image.' In our case, we can use SVG files (in Inkscape, Design Space, Photoshop, etc.) to make designs for Cricut to cut out.

Adaptive Tool System

One of the tools that can greatly enhance the capabilities of the Cricut Maker is the Maker's Adaptive Tool System. This system is only designed for the Maker model and can assist with controlling the Maker's tools (George, 2020). The Adaptive Tool System essentially uses mathematical algorithms and intricate brass gears to help make the Maker's cutting capabilities more precise.

Heat Transfer Vinyl (HTV)

When we refer to "Heat Transfer Vinyl," we're referring to the type of vinyl material that can be transferred on to project surfaces via heat transfer—ie. using the EasyPress to secure an iron-on vinyl to a project surface. The abbreviated version of "Heat Transfer Vinyl" is 'HTV.' In the same category (of vinyls), one of the main manufacturers of the HTV which we use for Cricut projects is Siser Easyweed, so if you come across a project that requires Siser Easyweed, they're simply referring to a brand of HTV.

Vinyls can also be differentiated by numbers such as 631, 651, or 951. The first category of vinyl is 631 Vinyl is simply 'removable' vinyl that is like a sticker. The 631 can be used for temporary wall art, window stickers, and other indoor objects that don't face a lot of external pressures such as the weather changes. There are two types of permanent vinyl, known as 651 and 951. The first Permanent Vinyl, the 651, is used for outdoor purposes and is waterproof, so it can be used to stick onto any surface that is exposed to the weather. The other vinyl category is the 951 Permanent vinyl. The 951 is marine-grade, meaning that it's stronger than the standard, permanent 651 adhesive capabilities (the higher the number, the stronger the grade of adhesiveness).

'Oracal' is one of the manufacturers of adhesive (stick-on) vinyls, such as the 631, 651, and 951 vinyls.

Thereafter, you get printable vinyls which is a sheet of vinyl that you can load into your inkjet or normal laser printer, you'll just need to ensure that the type of vinyl is the correct type for your printer. Generally speaking, printable vinyl is usually used with the "Print and Cut" function on Design Space.

The Weeding Tool

One of the more common terms that you'll come across when Cricutting is to 'weed' or to use your "weeding tool." The weeding tool is essentially a little pen-shaped tool with a needle-like head that you use to peel away any excess vinyl once you've cut your design with your Cricut. The weeding tool's main purpose is to mainly assist with vinyl projects. When Cricut instructions for projects tell you to "weed away any excess vinyl," you'll need to grab your weeding tool and carefully use the tool to pull out any excess vinyl that isn't part of the design. Alternatively, you can use tweezers or your fingers, but you'll have to be careful when it comes to the smaller and more intricate cuts and designs.

Carriage

In all of the Cricut machines, there is a compartment in the body called the 'carriage' where you can store your blades and other tools and accessories. The carriage moves back and forth along roller bars, like a cupboard drawer, so as to allow you easy access to your tools.

Cricut's Dial

On your Cricut machine (except for the Maker and the Joy), you'll find a little knob or dial that's used to select the material that you're going to be working with. You simply just adjust the dial to whichever material that you're working with and if you can't find that material option on the dial, you can choose the 'Custom' option and just select the material of choice in Design Space, prior to cutting. You'll have to choose the material before cutting, as well as set up the necessary blades, mat, and material into your machine.

Digital Cartridges

In Design Space, you may also come across the term "digital cartridges." Physical cartridges were needed for the older models of Cricut machines, but the newer models have removed the need for it, so, nowadays, you're more likely to see the term "digital cartridges" in replace of physical ones. Digital cartridges are essentially images that are grouped by something similar, such as an artist. However, the term "digital cartridges" was recently replaced with the name "image sets" now on Digital Space.

The Cricut's Rollers and Roller Bars

A few of the main functions on all of the models are their rollers and roller bars. The rollers and the small rubber wheels are near the entry where you load in your mat. It helps you to easily roll the mat and material into the machine without hassle. The roller bars are the two metal bars across the width of the machine that help the carriage move back and forth.

The bars also rotate to help the Cricut cut in any direction, with ease.

Star Wheels

ricut machines also come with Star Wheels that are little white gears that sit on the roller bars to help secure the materials to the mat. There are times when certain projects will ask you to consider shifting or adjusting the star wheels around, especially when you're cutting thicker materials with the Knife Blade.

While these are merely a few of the more common parts of your Cricut machine (and some tools for your toolkit), the range is ever-growing. The Cricut website is the best place to keep updated on the range of tools and accessories for your powerful, little machine and you can also peruse the catalog for any deals or promotions. There are hundreds of options for different styled and strengths of blades, as well as different styles and colors of pens available to build your glorious collection of Cricut accessories; thus, allowing you to continuously explore your range of project options and make the most unique end products!

Tools & Accessories for Your Cricut

In terms of understanding the physical body of your Cricut machine, we must first understand that aside from the physical body of the machine, the tools and accessories designed for each machine can exponentially enhance the capabilities and precision of the machine's cutting capabilities. For instance, understanding the types of blades and pens for different machines and materials can help the machine cut with much more efficiency and precision.

The Bonded Fabric Blade

The Bonded Fabric Blade is a blade that works with the Maker and Explore range, and it can be used to cut fabric with its blade backed with an ironed stabilizer to help stiffen it for support. The Bonded Fabric Blade comes in pink housing (the metal piece that holds the blade) and can help cut through tougher material or help with more intricate designs, due to its stabilized support system.

Types of Cricut Mats

Mats are another thing that you'll be making a lot of use of —it's required for any type of cutting to take place. The Cricut Joy is the only machine that can cut certain materials without the need for a mat. The mats are removable and have sort of an adhesive texture to it, so as to help the materials stay in place while the cutting process is happening. When you prepare your Cricut machine to cut, you'll need to load a mat into the machine along with your material of choice. Types of mats vary depending on the material that you're using (similar to the machine's blades). There are five types of mats: StandardGrip, LightGrip, FabricGrip, and the Cricut Joy Card Mat. The mats are based on the material type that you're using, what you need done (cutting, sewing, etc.) as well as the size of the design and machine. You can use your mat guide (the small, plastic guide) as a reference to help you properly insert the mat into the machine.

The Cricut Joy (the most recent addition to the Cricut family) has a considerably high amount of tools, accessories, and materials specifically designed for it. One of which is the Card Mat. The Card Mat is a mat that allows your Joy to quickly create cards by using pre-designed cards in Design Space. If you enjoy creating cards for others and you have the Joy, this can be a handy little tool to grab, to ease the card making and cutting process.

Smart Materials

The Cricut Joy doesn't only come with unique materials and tools, it can also work mat-less with some materials (unlike the rest of the Cricut range that requires a mat to cut). The Joy can work with materials known as 'Smart' materials (which are specifically created to work with the Joy), and come in forms of materials such as vinyls, infusible ink, and writable labels. The Joy can also cut much longer cuts without needing the traditional Cricut mat.

Fine Point Blade, Deep Cut Blade, and Knife Blade

The Deep Cut Blade comes in a black housing and works with the Cricut Maker and Explore machines. It's a blade designed to cut through much thicker materials such as leather and craft foam. The Fine Point Blade is a bit finer than the Deep Cut Blade, and the Cricut Maker's Knife Blade is a bit sharper. The Fine Point Blade comes in a silver or gold housing and is the standard blade in all of the Cricut machines, as it can cut through various materials such as paper, card stock, vinyl, etc. The Knife Blade is created specifically for use of the Maker and is used to cut through tougher material such as balsa wood, basswood, leather, chipboard, etc.

Perforation Blade

Another tool that's specific to the Cricut Maker is the Perforation Blade which, in its name, is self-explanatory. The Perforation Blade is simply used to help perforate lines into paper and cardstock which can greatly help with assembling pieces of a pattern together, for instance. The Rotary Blade is another tool specific to the Maker and is shaped like a small pizza cutter that can be used to glide through materials rather than dragging them when cutting. It's mainly used on tougher and thicker fabrics such as leather and felt, among other thicker fabrics.

Wavy Blade

The Wavy Blade is a tool specific to the Cricut Maker and can work with QuickSwap. It's one of the most exciting blades to add to your collection, especially if you like some funky patterns in your cuts! The Wavy Blade, as its name suggests, allows the machine to cut wavy lines into your material of choice, creating a groovy and smooth touch to your end project!

Debossing Tool

Another tool specific to the Maker is the debossing tool, and it's used to help create a gorgeous, embossed look in paper and cardstock! The tool can up your game in designing, creating, and cutting cards; if you're looking for a Cricut machine to help you create unique and custom cards, the debossed tool is a must-have in your tool kit!

Engraving Tool & Fabric Pen

Similar to the debossing tool, the Cricut Maker can also make use of the Engraving tool that can carve into surfaces such as acrylic or metal. In regards to fabrics, the Maker can also work with a tool called the Fabric Pen that works hand-in-hand with the Maker's rotary blade. The Fabric Pen can help ease the process of sewing, by creating little markings on the patterns once it's cut, so that you know where to stitch or match pieces together. Some people grab a pen holder and a few sharpies from their local store and use it in place of the Fabric Pen if they need a quick back up.

Aside from the Fabric Pen, all Cricut machines do come with a standard pen and holder, which can be instructed to write on different materials such as cards and papers. Cricut does offer a variety of pens and markers in different colors, styles, and types so that you have a plethora of options to choose from! There's also a new addition in the Maker model that allows you to easily make use of multiple tools instead of needing to constantly change the entire housing. With the Quick-Swap function, you just need to change out the tip of the tool by pressing on a plunger on the Maker, and then simply swap the tooltips! It's an amazing little addition that greatly enhances the capabilities and efficiency of the Maker.

Scoring Stylus

The Scoring Stylus is specifically used by the Maker and Explore range and is essentially a tool that creates a score in materials such as cardstock to create an easy line for folding. Similarly, the Scoring Wheel is only used by the maker and instead of only scoring the material like the Scoring Stylus, the Wheel drags across the cardstock (material) with its wheel to create a much deeper and more distinct line. The Scoring Wheel can come as a single wheel for easy scoring (for cardstock) or a double wheel for much deeper scoring on tougher, well-coated materials.

Making Stencils with Cricut Machine

Stencils are basically thin pieces of material with a design cut out of it, typically plastic, vinyl, or paper. This sheet is then placed on a flat surface such as a wall, furniture, etc., and then painted over. Only the cut-out parts of the stencil will allow paint to pass through, transferring the design on to the surface.

Material Needed in Making Stencils

- Cricut Machine
- Fine Point blade
- Standard Grip Machine Mat
- Access to Cricut's Design Software
- Weeding tools

Steps To Making Stencils With Cricut Machine

Making stencils with Cricut Machine is pretty easy. Here's how you can do it yourself.

- Firstly, you have to create and design your stencil using the Cricut's design software. Even as an amateur designer, there is a plethora of templates, fonts, and images available on the Cricut's designing software for you to choose from, so you don't even have to worry about being an expert designer. This way, it would be easy for you to print out your desired design.

So, choose what kind of design that you would want for your stencils, search for the design and then import it onto your design canvas. It is important to select designs with solid shapes; without stand-alone or broken lines.

- Once imported, proceed to adjust design settings such as size, orientation, etc. Ensure to arrange how your design will appear on your mat. The design software will automatically position your designs at the mat's edge; therefore, it is best to reposition this so that there is enough room to cut out your stencils.
- With the white part of the stencil vinyl in contact with the Standard Grip mat, load the Cricut machine with the stencil vinyl and then, proceed to cut it using the Cricut machine.
- Once the machine is done cutting, use your weeding tool to cut out your stencil designs. When completed, the stencil should be ready to be used on your desired surface.

- You can now use a foam pounce or other suitable material to apply paint through the stencil to design your wall or surface.

Making An Engraved Gift Tag Using Cricut Machine

An engraved gift tag can come in handy when you are looking to add a touch of personalization for your gift item to make it more special.

Materials Needed For Making An Engraved Gift Tag

- Strong Grip mat
- Masking tape
- A brayer
- An acrylic blank
- Access to Cricut's Design software

Steps In Making An Engraved Gift Tag

With the above-mentioned materials, you can proceed to prepare an engraved gift tag using the following steps.

1.) Designing Your Gift Tag:

- First, using the Cricut's canvas, select your desired design to be engraved. There are a combination of shapes, characters, text and templates that are available which you can utilize in creating your own design. The designs which work best with engraving are ones that are draw so ensure that the designs used are draw files.

- When you have finished creating your design, Click the attach tool and attach your designs so they appear on your acrylic blank the same way they appear on your design canvas, then select "Make it"

- You should then see a preview of where the design will be engraved on your mat. Make sure that it is positioned correctly —on your acrylic blank. If it isn't positioned satisfactorily, re-position it. Then click "Continue".

2.) Setting Your Acrylic Blank

- Firstly, remove the protective film from the front surface of the acrylic blank and then position it properly on the Strong Grip mat —not so close to the edge. When positioning the acrylic blank on the Strong Grip mat, make sure that it aligns properly within the measurements on the mat. Using a four-inch acrylic blank, it should be position to fit in between the 1-inch line and the 5-inch line bothering vertically and horizontally.

- When this is done, use the brayer flatten out the blank on the Strong Grip mat, so that it is stuck properly.
- Next, use the masking tape to firmly hold the blank in place. You do this by taping the acrylic blank edges onto the mat's surface. However, you should be careful not cover the part of the acrylic blank which you would want to engrave on with tape.

3.) Engraving Your Gift Tag:

- Proceed to set base material. You choose between one or two millimeters thick for the engraving depending the overall thickness of the acrylic blank which you're using.
- Once selected, you will be prompted to load your engraving tip in Clamp B on your Cricut Machine. Do so, and load your Strong Grip mat on to your machine to start engraving.

  When loading your mat, ensure to move the star rings from the way so they don't dent the acrylic blank. You can do this by sliding them over to the right- or left-hand side, depending on where your acrylic blank is. Press the arrow button on the machine to load your mat and then press the "C" button to start engraving.

- When this is done, your complete design on your blank's surface will be visible, you can go ahead and attach it onto desired surface.

Making Stickers With Cricut Machine

Materials Needed For Making Stickers

- Access to Cricut's Design Software
- A Cricut Machine (either Maker and Explore series)
- Printable Vinyl
- Light Grip Mat
- Fine Point blade

Steps To Make Stickers with Cricut Machine

1.) Designing The Stickers:

- Firstly, head over to Cricut's Design Software and design the stickers on the canvas. Since we'll be using Maker or Explore series to make these print then cut stickers, it is ideal to make these selections on your design software. At the top corner of the design software, select either of the explore or maker machines. If it's on Cricut joy, you should change it.

- Next, upload your stickers to the design canvas. When doing this, make sure that the background is removed. The stickers are going to have a checked background which indicates that there is no background. Print then cut image and then click upload. You should have your sticker ready to go.
- You can use the arrows to resize it to however you want, you can also duplicate it and make as many copies as you would like.
- Thirdly, you can proceed to click "Make It". Before you do so, make sure that all the stickers on your design canvas say print then cut over on the left-hand side of your screen.

Your stickers are now ready to print then cut your stickers using either you explore or maker machine.

Another thing to note is that the maximum size for print then cut is 6.75 inches by 9.25 inches. So, make sure that your entire stickers which you would be printing fit into this size. To do this, insert a square and resize it to 6.75 inches by 9.25 inches and then check to see whether your stickers fit into this shape on your canvas. If they don't, rearrange them in a way that they would, resize them or delete some of the duplicate stickers to create space for others. However, make sure that entire square space is utilized with the stickers so you don't waste materials.

2.) Printing And Cutting Your Stickers:

- Once you have arranged your stickers to fit into the space, delete the 6.75 by 9.25 inches square, select your entire stickers which you have arranged, and attach them using the Attach tool. This way, when you proceed to make it, they will all be on the same page exactly how you arranged them. Then you can proceed to print them.
- To print, click continue. Then click send to printer. When this is done, you will have to select the printer which you will use from the box at the top.
- Also, you can click to use the system dialog box before printing. This system dialog box would allow you to select a few preferences like paper type —matte paper setting, matte inkjet papers or matte presentation papers — and print quality. If the printer that you are using has a fast mode, you might want to turn that off. If everything else has been set, click okay and begin printing stickers.

- When the printing has been completed, you can then cut them using the Cricut machine. Take note that you wouldn't print on the grid side of the printable vinyl. Add the sheet to the Strong Grip mat by lining it up with the grid line and pressing it down well. Since we're using a mate sticker paper for this illustration, it should cut fine. If you're using a different kind of paper, and it's not cutting fine, take some matte finish tape —standard regular everyday scotch tape and apply them over those lines all around. This will make the Cricut machine cut your paper without the glare from the glossiness.

Another thing to note is that when using white paper to do print then cut, you can only use the Cricut Explore Air Two. When using colored papers, the Explore Three, Original Maker or Maker Three series are ideal. As only these three machines can print then cut with colored paper.

- Proceed to load the fine point blade into the Cricut machine, set the dial to custom and load your Strong Grip mat onto the machine by pressing the arrow button. Once it's loaded, press the go button to begin cutting all of the stickers.

- Once completed, unload the mat and detach the stickers easily. You can either remove the backing paper or remove the stickers directly, whichever one you'd want. Do you!

Cutting Shrink Plastic with A Cricut Machine To Make Photo Ornaments

Making photo ornaments with cut shrink plastic is a pretty easy project, this section is going to explain how you can do so with just your inkjet printer. There's no sublimation printer that is needed to carry out this project. With that being said, let's get right into it.

Materials Needed for Cutting Shrink Plastic and Making Photo Ornaments

- Cricut Machine Maker series or the Explore series: Maker 3, Explore Air 2, Explore 3, original Maker will work just fine.
- Shrink plastic: There's a printable version that prints in your inkjet printer and can be cut with your Cricut machine and then you can shrink it to make a sturdy plastic ornament for your holiday tree.
- A shrink film
- Strong grip mat.
- Deep point blade
- Brayer.

- An oven or a heat gun (to shrink the shrink film)
- Access to Cricut Design Space

Before proceeding, it is important to understand the different shrink film types.

The printable shrink film: Which is available in clear or in white colors. because it is clear and the Cricut machine cannot read the registration marks to cut the film itself, the clear shrink film will not cut on a Cricut machine. So, in this case, using the white version for this project is ideal. This is because it can be run through the inkjet printer, be printed right upon with the design and can be cut using the Cricut machine.

Steps To Cutting Shrink Plastic and Making Photo Ornaments

With all the needed supplies gone over, let's proceed to the designing software and look at how to design our photo ornaments because we're going to use our Cricut machine to cut this shrink plastic.

1.) Designing The Photo Ornaments:

We will go over three different ways with which you can make these ornaments.

- Firstly, you will need to import your images into Cricut Design Space, and you do that by clicking on the upload button and then you choose the image on your computer. Do that and upload the images for the ornaments. You're going to want to remove the background (if any) on the image so you can cut it as an ornament just the way it is.

- Since, the print then cut feature on Cricut Design Space is only 6.75 inches by 9.25 inches. So, you will need to resize the image using the arrow buttons to where it is less than that. The final size I came up with for this illustration is 6.59 inches by 9.223 inches.

Note that the package of shrink plastic used for this illustration says that it will shrink to 20% of the size which it is cut. If it's the same type of shrink plastic you're using, you're going to need to cut it really big to get an ornament that's any size. Since, the print then cut feature on Cricut Design Space is only 6.75 inches by 9.25 inches. So, you will need to resize the image using the arrow buttons to where it is less than that. The final size I came up with for this illustration is 6.59 inches by 9.223 inches.

- Next, make sure it says print then cut on the right-hand side of your design space and to do that, you will want to make sure that you have selected either the Maker or Explore series at the top right corner of the screen because the Cricut Joy does not do print then cut. So now, you should have your first ornament ready for cutting.

Alternatively, let's go over another method to resize the image that will be used for the ornament. In this next option, we're going use a hexagon to make this illustration.

- To draw a hexagon, use the shape feature on the Cricut's design software. Resize the hexagon to match the ornament, which is 7.762 by 6.721 for this project. That's also the maximum size you can make it.

- And then you just lay it over your picture in a location where it's covering the portion of the picture that you want. You can also resize your picture if you need to. And then you'll select the hexagon and the picture, then click Slice.

- Once that's done, go ahead to delete everything off except for your ornament now.

To further illustrate the difference between the first and second ornament, proceed to create a hole for the ribbon at the end of the second ornament (On the first ornament created in this illustration above, a hole punch will be used to add a hole).

- To create a hole to this one, click on shapes and insert a circle. Resize the circle to about 0.8 or so, 0.778 —that's okay and large enough so when it shrinks, a ribbon is still going to fit through it and they're going to pick them both.

- Also, you can do a line, center horizontally, and then Slice. Once done, proceed to delete off the circles that should leave us with a created ornament that has a circle inside.

So, this is one way a picture ornament can be made.

The third way which you can make these photo

ornaments is generally a combination of both methods already outlined.

- This can be done by, first, uploading the desired picture again, then, remove the background with the tool in design software and make a circle ornament that is 6.748 inches around which is the maximum size which could be made with this Cricut Machine.

- Proceed to add the ornament to the circle. You will have to make the circle white so the white of the shrink plastic will show through the ornament background.

- Then, copy this circle and paste it and drop another one down, then position the picture where you will want it to be on the circle, pick both and click slice.

- Lastly, delete everything except the image, then proceed to add the hole. You will have to insert a circle and make its size about 0.7-ish. Put those together, just pick the two circles, align, center horizontally on your circle, and then slice.

2.) Printing Your Ornaments:

By now, you should have a circle with a hole in it and your picture. Arrange and send it back with the circle and then, put those two over each other where they are aligned together.

- Select everything by clicking and dragging the cursor over everything and then click Flatten. Now you should have a print and cut ornament with a hole cut out of it. When printing your design, it should cut around the circle and cut a hole in the center. It will not cut around the image because it has been flattened.

- Proceed to click Make It and observe the options. Firstly, you will see a preview of the print and cut ornaments on the mat and you should proceed to check it to ensure that it looks okay. In this case, it is not necessary to mirror because you will print on top of your shrink plastic. So, click continue.

- Go ahead and send your stickers to the printer. Turn off bleed and, if your printer allows it, select a glossy paper setting from the system dialogue box. Proceed to print the ornaments you've designed and then they should be ready to cut.

For the material setting used for this illustration, click browse and search for "plastic". For cut settings, it is ideal for you to select plastic packaging. You can search for it. So, with this setting, it almost always cuts through the shrink plastic. However, you might have to do multiple passes for it to be completely cut through. How to do this will also be covered in this article.

3.) Cutting The Shrink Plastic:

So now you are ready for cutting, so proceed to the Cricut machine and cut the shrink plastic. With the ornaments all printed onto your shrink plastic film, dry the plastic film for about 5, 10 minutes right before you cut it, otherwise the ink will still be wet.

- To begin cutting, add the plastic film onto your Strong Grip mat. When doing this, you should line the plastic film up with the grids on the Strong Grip mat and then press it down firmly onto the Strong Grip mat. You can do this using the brayer, running it over the corners, and when you've confirmed that your ink isn't wet. Also, you can run it over the entire print, adhering it down to the Strong Grip mat. Once that has been done, you are now ready to begin cutting. So, head over to the Cricut machine and cut the shrink plastic film.

- Ensure that the Deep Point blade has been added to the Cricut machine. You can do this by putting it into the clamp and then you'll want to move the White Star Wheels on the Cricut machine all the way to the right side of machine. This is ideal so as not to drag the star wheels though the wet ink.

- Once the Cricut machine is ready, Press the arrow button to load the Strong Grip mat onto the Cricut Machine.

- With the Strong Grip mat loaded, press the "C" button to cut. The machine will first detect the registration marks on the Shrink Plastic Film in order to ascertain where it is going to cut and then the machine will proceed to cutting the design. When the cut is done, you should check assess the cut to confirm whether the machine has completely cut through the shrink film. Start lifting up the shrink plastic and see if it's cut through. However, do not unload it from the machine.

- Usually, you can redo the cutting process all over with your machine a few more times just to ensure that it has been cut through. Press the arrow button to redo the process and begin another round of cutting. Just be sure to pause the cut intermittently and confirm whether it has completely cut through.

- When you have noticed that it is indeed cut-through. Proceed to unload the Strong Grip mat and then start removing the Shrink Plastic Film from the Strong Grip mat. You can do this by turning the mat over and then peeling it back from the Shrink Film.

While the machine is cutting the Shrink film, the Deep Point blade can get pretty jammed with the plastic. So, it is ideal that you pause the Cricut machine intermittently, get the debris removed from the blade, even push it out and sort of clean it off and then insert it again into the Cricut machine. Also, when the cutting is done, you'll notice that the machine does make little white specks of the plastic get all over your project. Try to get as many of those off as possible because as the plastic melts, those little pieces can kind of get embedded in and make your project appear speckle. So, you can just wipe them down before shrinking them.

For the pieces completely cut out, some will have a circle at the top which was added while designing on the design software. For those pieces that don't have, you will need to punch a hole before you shrink it, since it won't be possible to punch the hole after the shrinking is complete. A hole punch can be used to create a hole in any of the pieces without the holes at the top.

4.) Shrinking The Plastic:

There are multiple ways to shrink the plastic, which will be explained below. We will also go over an alternate method to do it.

This first method of shrinking plastic will use an oven and according to the directions on the package of the shrink plastic used for this illustration, we're going to do 350 degrees for two to three minutes. If you're using a different brand, please follow those instructions.

- So, firstly, line the tray that comes with the oven with parchment paper. Then, put the straight plastic down and then cover that with a sheet of parchment paper. This top will keep it from curling too much and sticking to itself.

- Next, head over to the oven, put it inside and watch it shrink. You can preferably set your timer for three minutes. Then you will see, as the shrink plastic heats, it will curl up. It will curl up significantly and you will think that it's going to stick to each other, but in the end, it flattens back out and you have a cute ornament.

- After right at two minutes, the ornament has completely shrunk. You can go ahead and take it out of the oven.

- Once the ornaments are out of the oven, put it on a flat surface and use a heat resistant glove to press down from the top while the ornament cools. This makes it as flat as possible and then you have your ornaments completed. Once the ornaments are cool, you can remove them from the parchment paper and then you can see the photo ornaments ready.

For the alternate method to shrink the plastic, a lot of people use it as well. It generally involves using a heat gun and a heat resistant mat, like the Easy Press mat.

- To do use this method, put your shrink plastic on the mat and start heating it up with the heat gun. And it will shrink. You will need something like Popsicle sticks or something to kind of hold it flat because it would curl up onto itself and kind of make a jumbled ornament.

Ornaments made using this method usually have ridges and it may be difficult to get consistent heating or a completely flat surface with this method.

- Now, all that's left to do is just string some ribbon onto each of these, tie it into a knot, and hang it on the tree.

Now, you can have your completed photo ornament with an inkjet printer and my Cricut machine and shrink plastic.

Making A Birthday Card With Cricut Machine

Handmade birthday cards are a really creative and personalized way of celebrating a friend's birthday or any other special occasion. This section discusses how you can make a birthday card with your Cricut machine all by yourself. Let's go right into it!

Materials Needed To Make A Birthday Card

- Access to Cricut design space
- Cricut Machine: The Cricut Maker 3 will be used for this illustration. However, since this project uses the fine point blade which comes with every Cricut machine, you can as well use other Cricut machine types for this project.
- A variety pack of cardstock

- The Light Grip mat: This usually comes with most Cricut machines except the Explore 3 or the Maker 3. So, if you're using any of these machines, you might want to look for a 12x12 light grip mat that is blue in color.
- Glue or adhesive: This will be necessary to put the card together.
- A scoring stylus or scoring wheel
- A spatula: This tool is great for getting small paper pieces off your mat but is not essentially required for this project.
- A brayer: This as well is great for the project because it extends the life of your mat. It helps to firmly push down your paper into the adhesive when you lay your paper on the mat.

Steps To Make A Birthday Card

1.) Designing The Card:

The first step to making a birthday card is to create or find your design for the birthday card.

- You can easily do this on the Cricut design space by searching for "birthday" or "birthday cards" and then a variety of design templates would come up, then select your preferred design. As a beginner, choosing a simple card design with just one- or two-color combinations is recommended. That way you can get a feel for your machine before you dive into more complicated cards.

For the purpose of this illustration, we will be using a simple design that comes with an envelope. When you do so, you'll notice on the layers panel that it comes in group. So, you'll want to ungroup it to tweak the colors a little bit more. That way, when you proceed to make it, you will be able to visualize the final project on the screen and you will be given a clue as to the colors you've decided to use.

- So, to tweak the colors, pick the selected card, make sure to pick just the cut and click the drop-down menu to choose a different color for the card. For advanced colors or if you want to pick a specific shade, click the plus sign (+) beside advanced to do that. You would want to pick a color that is close to or matches the color paper you're going to use. You can also pick your desired color for the envelope as well.
- Then make sure that the proper machine is picked for your project on Cricut Design Space. To do this, pull down the menu at the top of your design space and pick the machine that you're using.

Now, any Cricut machine can cut paper, so you can definitely pick from any of the machines that you have.

- Resize the card. If you click on the card, you will see its size. You can use a physical ruler to visualize what it will look like and also when it is folded. If you are not okay with it and you want to resize your elements, there's two ways to easily do that:
- The first way, click and drag your cursor over the area

to completely cover your elements on your canvas and then make sure the lock button is locked, then use the arrow button to resize them. This will change all elements at the same amount, maintaining their proportions.

- The second way, you could select an element and then type in your preferred size. Then proceed to cut.

2.) Settings For Cutting Your Project:

- Using the Maker 3, this project can be cut on the on the mat using regular paper. So, to do that, select on mat, and then click done. You should see all of the elements and they will look exactly the same and then click continue.

- Connect your machine and have it switched on and then proceed to pick card stock. On Cricut card stock, there is usually a Cricut C beside that indicates their brand of material, so you can definitely browse all materials if you want to see more options for your material type and you can even type the name of the material into the search box.

- Once you've selected the card stock you want to use for the project, go ahead and pick the appropriate settings. The medium cardstock setting is ideal for this project. If you have really small cuts, the cardstock for intricate cuts settings is what you would use. Although, it is not recommended to have small cuts for starter projects. Once you've chosen your settings, click done.

- Next, it will be indicated that you need a scoring wheel. So, you are going to score the envelope and card to get those fold lines. If you have the scoring stylus instead, you would click edit tools, and you could pick scoring stylus from the menu and click apply. You can do that in both cases for the envelope and the card, just depending on what scoring tool you have. Then it will tell you to put your scoring stylus in this case in clamp A and the fine point blade in clamp B.

- Now, if you have the single scoring wheel, pick it and load it in clamp B, the machine would score. Then, it would stop and the software would ask you to load your fine point blade, then you do it and then it would cut your envelope or your card. So, you can make this whether you have the stylus or the scoring wheel. So now let's head to the Cricut and cut a card.

3.) Cutting Your Project:

- Before cutting, the first thing you're going to want to do with your mat is to peel back the protective sheet and then save it because you'd want to store your mats with the sheet attached to keep dirt and debris off of your mat and make them last a little bit longer.

- Then you're going to cut the white paper first. To do this, use the grid lines on the mat to line up your paper and once it's lined up, just press it down into that adhesive. You can use the brayer here by rolling it across the paper to press it down even more and then you have your paper ready for the machine.

- At this point, the arrow button should be flashing on your machine indicating that you're ready to load your mat. So, you take your mat to your machine, make sure it's under the guides on both sides, press it against the rollers and hold it up against the rollers while and press down the arrow button at the same time. This will load the mat into the machine. The machine will check that you have the correct blade installed and that you have enough material.

- Once loaded completely, press the go button and the machine will cut the design. When the machine is done cutting, the arrow button will start flashing again and then you press it to unload your mat. Then, you will see that the project is cut.

For the scoring stylus, since it is a little more common, open clamp A for the stylus, make sure the arrow and the word Cricut on your stylus is facing you. Put that into your machine and press down until it clicks and then you just close the clamp and then the stylus is ready to use. With the fine point blade in clamp B for the cutting portion, it will score and cut. All you have to do is press the go button one time.

Then, load your mat in the same way and then just press the go button to cut. The machine will add the scoring lines first and then it will cut the rest of your project. Once it's done cutting, go ahead and remove the mat from the machine and remove the paper from the mat as well. Then, go ahead and cut the second pink sheet with the card.

4.) Unloading and Removing Your Paper:

A very efficient tip for removing paper from a Cricut mat is to do it the opposite of the conventional way.

- To do that, turn your mat over upside down and peel the mat back from your project instead of the other way around. This is better because, the paper does not curl as badly and as you go along, you can pull out all your little pieces which, in this case, would be scrap.

5.) Assembling the project

- With the score line running down the middle which was added by the Cricut machine it's super easy to find. Using it, fold the card exactly in half.

- Then add your preferred adhesive or glue on the back of your birthday design. Then once you have that added, just add your paper to the front of your card, lining it up exactly with the card front and then press your adhesive into place and the card itself is done.

- You can now write any sentiment you would like on the inside.

Now to make the envelope that goes along with it, all you need to do is fold along the score lines. There should be four score lines, so, run the adhesive along to hold three flaps together and then press down to glue.

This should give you an envelope which you can add your already made card. Then, close the flap, and it's ready to give.

Making Earrings with Cricut

Making earrings with Cricut machine is another fun project which you would love to try out. These homemade earrings, if done properly, are equally as fashionable and can cost way lesser than you may think because they only require simple household supplies. So, let's first examine the supplies that we will be needing for this project.

Materials Needed for Making Earrings With A Cricut Machine

- Access to Cricut design space
- Faux leather: This is recommended instead of genuine leather just for the weight of the earrings.
- A standard grip mat.

- Some jewelry findings such as the hooks for your earring as well as matching jump rings, jewelry pliers and a tool to punch a hole on the top. You would want to use this instead of cutting a hole with the Cricut machine.

- Your Cricut machine

Steps To Make an Earring Using Your Cricut Machine

1.) Designing Your Earrings

This is carried out on the Cricut Design Space so you'll want to head over there and take a look at the earrings.

- The first thing you'll need is your file to cut. So, you can add the free SVG into Cricut Design Space just by uploading. If the uploaded SVG file is grouped, you will have to ungroup them and separate the pieces. This way, you can pick and choose which ones you want to cut. If you want to cut them out of different materials, you would need to change the colors so they go onto different mats.

- Now, you can also click images right in Cricut Design Space and search for earrings in the corner and you can also find some cut files that are Cricut cut files which you might need to pay for to cut those earrings as well.

- Once you have earrings in Cricut design space, the next thing we put up is the faux leather. The faux leather can be just a little scrap piece which is small but useful as long as you can still cut earrings out of them. So, put the faux leather face down on the mat. This means that you will need to mirror the cuts if your earrings are not symmetrical.

So go ahead and mirror that cut before cutting and then we're proceed to cut it on the Cricut machine.

2.) Cutting Your Material

- For the Explore series, set your material to custom. Make sure you have your mirror on and they're sized perfectly to your preferred size. With the material set on custom, click browse and type faux and then faux leather. This is to allow you to select the appropriate material which you are cutting. This process is exactly the same if you're using the Maker series, you don't have to turn the dial, the Maker will automatically pull up the list.
- Next, you will be prompted to insert the fine point blade. Once done, you can load your mat and then start your cut.
- Then once it's done, you just unload it and then you can remove the faux leather from your mat and remove our earrings. Also, you could turn both of them into a set of earrings by inserting a hole and the hooks on them.

So now that they're cut and assembled, you now have

your finished earrings.

The Cricut Maker 3

This is the latest in the models of the Cricut machines. This version is an upgrade to the famous Cricut Maker machine. The look and design have been completely changed, starting from the top to the bottom, with an improved work rate and speed that is twice that of the Maker and more powerful.

The Maker 3 name given to this latest model signifies the same technological features as the Cricut Explore 3.

This electrically operated device can make cuttings on a vast amount of materials, over 300. It has a smart tool system that enables the user to gain control of 13 various tools, making switches of the tips to perform several functions, specifically to cut, deboss, draw, score, engrave and foil different materials.

Features and Functions of Maker 3

The features of the Maker 3 are an upgrade and update to that of the Maker model. With this, you're accomplishing more tasks and saving time. The appearance is quite similar.

One ideal feature that differentiates the Cricut Maker 3 from that of other models is the smart tool system which possesses unique properties. It comprises 13 tools performing several functions: to make cuts, deboss, score, engrave, and more.

With the QuickSwap feature, you can easily swap the tools head. It is an attachment system consisting of two different clamps identified with labelings A and B. With this, you can accomplish two different tasks in one work.

Smart Materials have been included. These materials: Smart Vinyl, Smart Paper, Smart Iron-on, 13" wide, enable the Cricut Maker 3 to make long length cuts of 12 feet without a mat. All it takes is loading the Smart Materials, then proceed.

With the Maker 3, you can perform tasks with an excess of 300 materials, which can be in the form of silk-like materials, cotton, and cashmere, and leather, wood, and denim, which are quite strong. It can also work on materials like vinyl, which can be difficult for laser cutters.

Using the Iron-On Smart Material and an iron, you can attach the material to the fabric.

This technique can be applied to T-shirts. It is of various colors.

The Maker 3 can slice materials up to 330 mm wide and 3,600 mm long. In any case, to arrive at that, the roll holder is quite handy. This holder can accommodate vast rolls of vinyl and iron-on, keeping them in position during cutting.

The cutting speed of the Cricut Maker 3 is increased to twice that of the Maker model. It cuts up to 8 inches in a second, cutting smart materials.

The Cricut Maker 3 has the Design Space software to get your images and designs uploaded onto the machine. It works with file formats such as: .jpg, .png, .bmp, .gif, .svg, and .dxf.

The Maker 3 is a device of compact size that should fit well into spaces without any problem.

How to use the Cricut Maker 3?

The Cricut Maker 3 is automated and controlled by a software. There is a regular update on the Cricut software, so a brand new Maker 3 might require a couple of updates on firmware.

This is possible with the use of the Internet. The incredible thing about the Cricut Maker 3 is that it can associate with the Internet both by means of a wired connection, that is, using a USB connected to a computer Bluetooth connection, which is wireless. After setting up and updating the firmware, proceed to the Cricut Design Space page.

Open the application and sign in utilizing your Cricut ID. You will be taken to Design Space's illustrations design interface, and this is where you can make essentially anything you desire, from banners to cards and T-shirt models.

The Cricut Maker 3 has several tools, and they were made given specific purposes. Basically, you need to pick the right tool for a task, so if you're drawing, a pen is useful, and if you're cutting, go with a good blade.

To begin the process of making cuts, place the mat for

cutting in the machine. Take away the mat cover. Then lay the material over the cutting mat while ensuring it impeccably holds fast to the surface. Both mat and material are loaded into the machine whenever you are done.

Have it in mind that you can as well save time by utilizing Smart Materials, as there's no need for a cutting mat. This implies that you can stack the material into your Cricut Maker 3 machine to kick it off.

Then, press the "Make It" button in the upper right corner, and you can begin cutting into your ideal materials.

Cricut Explore 3 vs. Cricut Maker 3

Both machines come as the latest installments from Cricut™, with the same outlook or duplicate as the Cricut Maker and the Cricut Explore Air 2. In terms of size, Maker 3 and Explore 3 are similar. The same goes with how productive they are and also, same kind of tools and materials, which can be interchanged. You can equally use both machines for the same type of projects, with a good outcome, so it can be difficult to pick between the two.

Well, two things are being looked out for by most crafters: good versatility and outstanding growth. Look no further as the Cricut Maker 3 can easily give you these. But if you're more concerned with having a smaller amount of financial investments or involvement in your craft, the Explore 3 is ideal. It is less expensive and performs well as the Cricut Maker.

There's a major difference between both machines: the cutting technology. The Maker 3, together with other machines in the same line, has the Adaptive Tool System. This system makes it possible for the Maker 3 to craft with 13 tools, more advanced than the Explore 3 with only six tools. You can write, cut, score, foil, debs, and do more functions using the Maker 3 tools. For Explore 3, the tools are limited to cutting, writing, and foiling.

Setting Up Your Cricut Machine

How to Set Up Your Cricut Machine

Some easy steps to follow in setting up your Cricut machine.

- The Cricut machine works with electricity. Plug the machine into a power source.
- Press the power button to get the machine turned on.
- There are two options for you to connect the machine to your computer. It is either you use the USB cable or via Bluetooth for wireless access.
- Go to your updated browser and open it.

- Go to Cricut's website, www.cricut.com/setup.
- Select Get started.
- You'll see your device from the list. Select it.
- Click on Download.
- The Setup will get downloaded to your system.
- Look for the Install.exe file in your downloads folder. Double click on it to kickstart the installation process. An installation setup window will come up.
- Do ensure you're signed in to your account for Cricut.
- Follow up with prompted instructions as they guide you through setting up your Cricut machine.

You can immediately begin work on your first project, presented with a step-by-step guide.

Setup is eventually completed when you're prompted to perform a test cut.

Cricut Maker 3 with Bluetooth Guide

- Your machine is Bluetooth enabled and comes with a wireless Bluetooth adapter. Insert into the machine.
- Ensure your computer is Bluetooth enabled

also. Go to Device Manager after clicking on the Start menu to check for this. Look for Bluetooth, and if found, then your system is enabled. If not, there's a need to purchase a Bluetooth Dongle.

- Go to Settings. Click on Devices.
- The Bluetooth should be turned on. Then, click Add Bluetooth.
- Create a connection between your computer and the machine.
- Input 0000 as PIN when prompted.
- Click on the Connect option.

Pairing the Machine with a Mobile device

- Setup the Cricut machine with all units intact and plugged into a good power source. Switch it on.
- Create a connection between your computer and the machine with Bluetooth.
- Go to App Store on your smartphone.
- Using the search bar, search for the Cricut application and install it.
- After installation, open the app, and with your Cricut ID, sign in.

- From the menu, tap on Machine Setup.
- The Cricut model in use will be displayed. Tap on it.
- The next set of instructions are guides to complete the setup.

Resetting the Cricut Maker 3

There is a need for the machine to undergo a reset when certain errors are encountered. This reset serves as a solution to sun issues. The following steps can perform a hard reset.

- Switch off the Cricut Maker 3.
- At the same time, hold down the following buttons: the one below Menu, that directly above Menu, and Power.
- This should be done until you observe a rainbow screen. Release the buttons immediately.
- The machine gives you directions to follow to complete the reset process.

Latest Version of Cricut Design Space

The release of the Cricut Maker 3 comes with an updated version of the Design Space - version 6.0. This is an improved version with enhanced features.

Choosing Material Settings

You can easily choose the kind of material settings you want after your Cricut Maker 3 has been successfully connected to your computer or mobile device. The material settings are seen to have a series of tiles. Choose a particular setting and click on the tile to select.

Custom Cut Settings of the Cricut Maker 3

You have a wide range of materials to choose from for your craft, and the Cricut Maker 3 availability gives a perfect fit for craftworks. Different pre-programmed settings have been added to the Design Space, offering you lots of flexibility when carrying out tasks.

To create custom material settings:

- Get access to the account created for Design Space and open a project.
- Your Maker 3 should be powered on and connected to the computer beforehand.
- Go to the Project Preview screen.
- You'll see Browse All Materials.
- After selecting the above, take a look at the list. Scroll to look through. The search option is available if you know the material by name. Some materials have the Cricut logo by the side. These are branded

materials from Cricut.

How to Create a New Custom Material?

It is possible that a material is not in the Custom materials list. There are two options for you to try: the closest matching settings or just go about creating one. To do this:

- First of all, open the Custom Materials screen from the app menu. You can either choose to Manage Custom Materials or go directly to Material Settings. The Settings are seen down the page when scrolling through the available materials suitable for your project.
- At the end of the list, there's the Add New Material option. Select it.
- Indicate the name of the new material and then save it.
- Adjustments can be made to the saved material.

Cut Pressure: **adjusted by using the slider or the +/- buttons.**

Multi-cut: **The machine makes several cuts on an image with this option. This goes well with materials of thicker nature.**

Blade Type: you got to choose your ideal blade. After necessary configurations, save all changes.

- The X button is at the top right of the screen to close the screen. Check the list of materials for the newly created material.

Installing the Bluetooth Adapter to the Cricut Machine

- Assemble and switch on the Cricut machine.
- Take off the covering on the Bluetooth Adapter.
- Plug in the adapter into the correct opening on the machine. The inscription "Cricut" should be facing up.
- About 2/3rd of the adapter should go in.
- A blue light at the end of the adapter indicates that it is in place.

Cricut Maker 3 Tools and Accessories Needed

Cricut Knife Blade

The Cricut knife blade is well suited for craft materials of a very thick nature. It is designed with an extra-deep blade capable of cutting through denser structure materials measuring up to 2.5mm. Some materials with such nature are matboard, balsa wood, and chipboard.

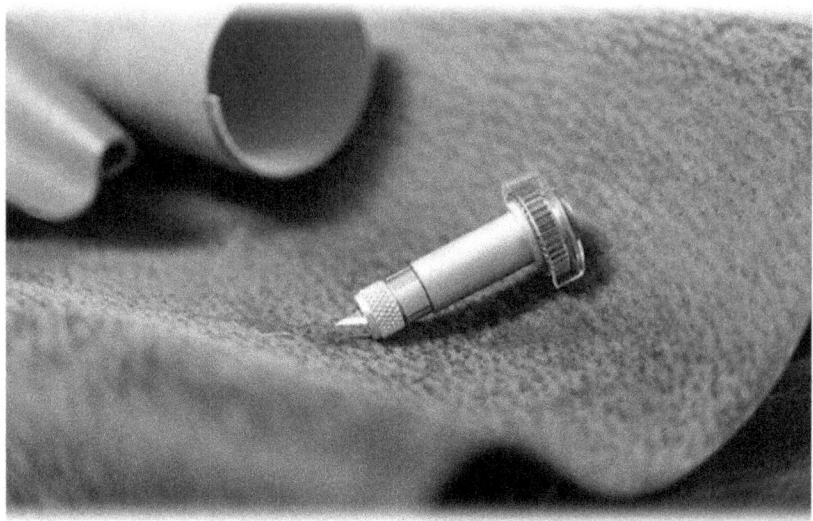

Cricut Rotary Blade

This blade comes along with the Cricut Maker 3 and performs great jobs on projects it is used. It can be applied to different fabrics, felt, and quilt batting.

On usage, it can last for a very long time and maintain its sharp quality, but using it for lots of projects involving fabrics, felts, and other materials can reduce its quality, making it a need to be replaced.

Cricut Mat

The Cricut Maker 3 has been designed without mats and doesn't come with one. It is designed to work with Cricut Smart Materials such as vinyl, iron-on, and cardstock, without needing a mat.

Well, projects are of various kinds and require different materials to work with, so a project to be executed may need other materials that are not Smart Materials. This case requires a mat to be purchased, which must be ideal for the material.

Scoring Stylus or Scoring Wheels

Projects such as cards, boxes, envelopes, and 3D paper works are to be folded during the course of making them. The application of Scoring gives a brilliant outlook to these craft forms.

The Scoring Stylus can be interchanged with that of the Scoring Wheel. Also, you can place both in Clamp A of the machine to make fold lines on your crafts.

Cricut Pen

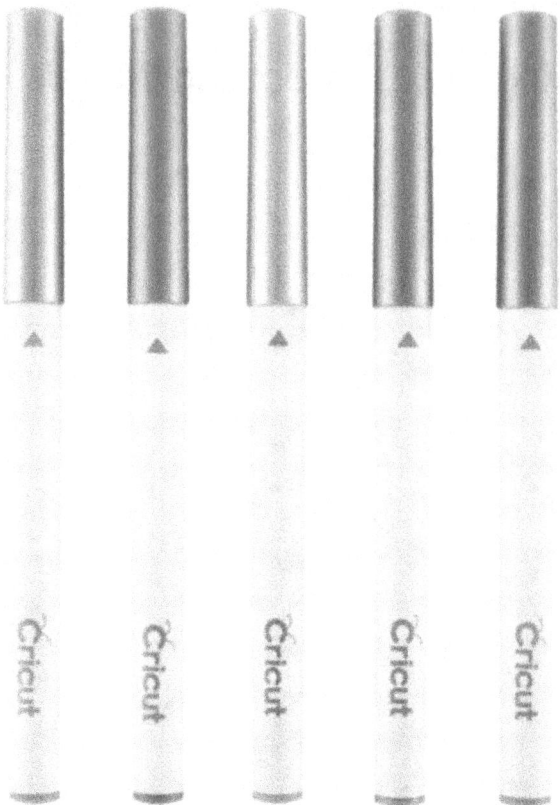

The Cricut pens are ideal for creating different shapes and writing beautiful texts on projects. You can also use them to design great cards and coloring books.

These pens contain no acid, devoid of toxic substances, and remain permanent on the project after it has been well dried for 24 hours.

Cricut Fabrics Pens

In a case where you cut out sewing patterns using the Cricut machine, the cutting and marking of the pieces are done simultaneously.

Cricut Roll Holder

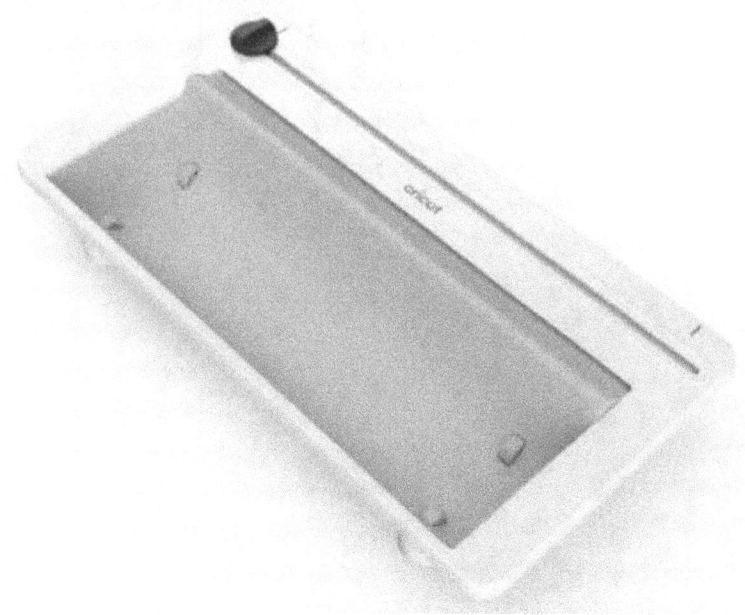

One amazing feature of the Cricut Maker 3 is the ability to cut up to 12 feet in length when using Smart Materials, thus limiting the need for a roll holder. There's no need to purchase a roll holder for the rolls of Smart Materials, but it, in a way, helps to keep the material well-positioned when cutting.

Brayer and Removal Tool

Want a smooth fabric or material? The brayer tool is useful. It smoothens down the fabric on the mat to get rid of air bubbles or wrinkles. This tool can be used for other materials, like vinyl or cardstock.

Cricut Smart Materials

Using the Smart Materials come with ease. You just need to load them into the Cricut machine and press Go.

Smart Materials usually consist of various material types. Materials that are quite common are Cricut Smart Iron-On, Cricut Smart Cardstock, and Cricut Smart Vinyl.

Adhesive Vinyl

This vinyl comes with lots of benefits when used. It is a good product to have. It can be applied to crafts such as glassware decoration, sign making, and projects centered on home decor.

Adhesive vinyl is of different specialties with an array of colors.

Heat Transfer Vinyl or Cricut Iron-On

Iron-On Vinyl, otherwise known as Heat Transfer Vinyl (HTV), is one very common product applied to different fabrics such as shirts, aprons, and tote bags. Wood and metal are not left out as they also work well with the product.

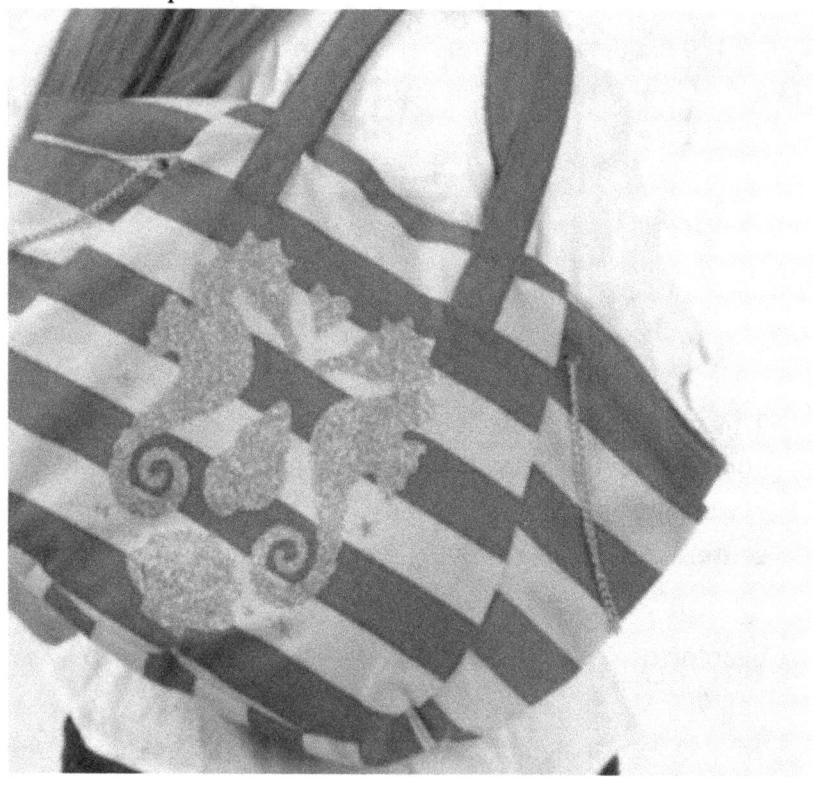

Paper and Cardstocks

Projects done using paper or cardstock are ideal for beginners or starters. They are more of essential materials and are quite cheap. Working with these materials comes easy, and mistakes encountered during use can easily be corrected.

How to Change Cricut Machine Blade

Crafting processes or the making of projects require different materials, and they, in a way, affect the Cricut machine blades, in which they need to be changed. Changing blades can be done at intervals or if the cuts are no longer as swift or crisp as before.

To change your machine blades:

- Take off the blade housing from the machine on opening the Clamp B.
- Remove the covering of the new blade. The covering serves as a protective cover.
- The new blade then goes right into the housing. There is a magnet inside, which helps to keep the new blade in position.
- The blade housing is then returned to its position, that is, Clamp B. Close it after that.

How to Cut Lightweight and Heavyweight Materials

Materials that are less than 3/32 of an inch or measuring 2.4mm thick can easily be cut by the Cricut Maker. There is a comparison between the new knife blade it carries and the X-ACTO knife with great precision cuts.

The machine is designed with a rotary blade that can make cuts when pushed down and roll along the material. The result is smooth, clean, and precise cuts, even on delicate designs.

Start with creating your design or pattern using the Design Space to make cuts. Then proceed to the Make It button.

Load the material into your machine after pressing the Load/Unload button. Click on the Go button. The machine goes ahead with the cutting.

How to Design, and Various Best Suited Materials

The Cricut Maker 3 is incapable of working independently without the Design Space being active. To get started, launch the Design Space and begin a new project. The Design Space comes with numerous designs and projects you can work with, and they are free. You just need to take up one and proceed with it.

It is great if you want to make your custom project by starting afresh from the beginning. Design Space provides you with a huge collection of elements to create such designs. Also, you are provided with the option of uploading an SVG file containing a design, and the machine cuts up the work.

Numerous projects, designs, fonts, and illustrations are all free to use in the Design Space, but having an access membership offers more benefits.

How to Clean Cricut Machine (Clamps, Rear rod, Outside of your Cricut Machine)

Prolonged use of your machine can accumulate dust

and paper particles. There may be observed grease build-up on the carriage shaft in other cases. The process of cleaning is very easy.

You must switch off your machine and unplug it from the powers source before you take part in cleaning.

- The machine is first opened, and the blade housing moved towards the left through the metal rod. Take off the blades together with the attachment from the clamp.

- Get air into the machine using a pressurized air can. Blow air over the internal compartments and ensure it gets to underneath the trays, clamps, and side caddies. You should also concentrate on the teeth at the back of the machine.

- Get alcohol and baby wipes without bleach. Use it to clean off areas that are seen to be dirty.

- Roller stars on metal rods are moved to a particular position. This provides an opportunity to have access to in-between and under the rods with a soft brush of small size. After you're done with dusting that area, move the tool housing from its position to the left side to have access to underneath are. While moving the tool housing from the initial position, do It slowly and without jerking. Also, pushing it too far and over can cause an altercation in the machine's functioning. Check the metal bars and the areas between them. Clean such areas and do well not to come in contact with the tool housing chain. After dusting the area, place back the blade attachment in position.

- The soft, brittle brush can have dust particles kicked up during cleaning. To clean these particles off the metal bars, go over using baby wipes. The rods come with lubricants and so shouldn't be cleaned off. Concentrate on the ends of the rods. These ends accumulate more dust as the oil serving as lubricant gather at that point. Spread the build-up of oil over the rod with a flathead brush. Wipe off any lubricant seen on the side of the machine with baby wipe.

- Lubrication helps keep gears running, but for the Cricut, there's no need to smear grease on the rods. If there's a need for your machine to be lubricated, Cricut's support team will be of help. Contact them for evaluation of the machine. You'll be sent a special kit with specific instructions on applying the lubricant.

- There must be due consideration on the type of brush used in between the tool housing. Use a brush with soft bristles and a round head. Take off the adapter and clean the clamp with the brush. During the process of cleaning the adaptive tool system, it is ideal you work gently. Ensure you use the ideal brush, not just any brush or cloth. Pressurized air should be used for delicate compartments.

- Give the machine some time to dry after making use of baby wipes. On drying, get a microfiber cloth to dust take off any dust remaining on the inside of the machine.

- Complete the cleaning by spraying air duster over the machine. Place back the star wheels into position, with the same amount of space in between.

- Switch the machine on finally. The housing unit reset itself.

How to Clean the Outside of Your Cricut Machine?

When making projects, your machine can gather dust particles and materials when cutting. To clean off these particles:

- Make use of a gentle cleaner on the surface. When cleaning the buttons on the machine, ensure that the quantity of chemicals used is little. Too much chemical or liquid can cause damages to the parts. For scuff marks, add some cleaner on a paper towel and rub over such marks.

- After you are done with the marks, clean over the machine with baby wipes. Take care not to tamper with the cartridge slot.
- Dry the machine with a paper towel to get rid of excess liquid.
- A microfiber cloth is then used to wipe the machine. This helps to take off any remaining particles or residue.
- Pass pressurized air over all the crevices seen on the machine's surface to dust off particles. The gaps at the bottom and connection ports should particularly be concentrated on as they are prone to dust accumulation.
- After opening the machine, use your round head brush to wipe the back gap along the bottom. Take note; you're doing this from the inside. Spray some pressurized air over the front side of the machine to expel dust particles from the back of the machine.

How to Design On Cricut Maker 3

How to Make Use of Sure Cuts

Sure Cuts A Lot (SCAL) is a program every beginner will find useful for making projects or craftworks. This program makes it easy to cut fonts and shapes of different sizes with a cutting machine. You can create custom designs or make combinations of fonts and other available shapes, patterns, or designs.

Many users go for the Sure Cuts, and it's quite obvious. There's a need for an active internet connection to practically work with Design Space, either for cutting projects or making designs. With SCAL, you can do designs offline, making it one big advantage over the Design Space.

How to Connect Sure Cuts A Lot (SCAL) to Cricut

To make the connection:

- Launch the SCAL software on the computer system.
- Switch on the Cricut machine.

- Assemble the paper to be used on the cutting mat.
- Access the menu and go to Cutter from the options. This allows you to choose your preferred size mat.
- With the Design Space software, users can easily transfer images from other sources into the Space and make them cuttable. The SVG file or graphics works well on the Design Space platform. Just transfer the SVG file from the SCAL into the Design Space.
- Transferring the SVG file from your computer starts with clicking the +SVG button.
- Sure Cuts A Lot program offers you access to freestyle drawing tools. It is seen as the only software to offer these. Both Mac and Windows platforms support the SCAL software.

Features of Sure Cuts

- SCAL supports already installed TrueType and OpenType fonts. Not only that, it can work well with other numerous fonts available on the other file formats are supported by the SCAL, not only SVG files. Files that can be imported are PDF, AI, EPS,

WPC. The PRO version of the program supports that of PLT and DXF. You can also work with embroidery file formats such as PEC, PES, HUF, SEW, VIP.

- It comes with Auto tracing to change images to cuttable forms.
- Different drawing tools for making drawings and editing shapes.
- Welding tool to weld shapes and letters together.
- There are a couple of special effects such as Drop Shadow, 3D Rotate, Knockout, Symmetrical Mirror, Puzzle Generator, Wave, and others.
- Numerous styles you can choose from to give your letters and shapes a different look, for example, Shadow and Blackout.
- Make rhinestone templates.
- Supported by Windows and Mac OSX.
- Access to free technical support.

Using Design Space

The Design Space affords you great features to shape up, beautify, edit, and organize your designs as a user. You do not only create and upload your custom font and images, but have access to make use of premium images and fonts from Cricut through purchase, Cricut

Access Membership, and Cartridges.

Top Panel Cricut Design Space

The Design Space Canvas or interface has a top panel containing design elements for editing and organizing designs on canvas. This panel allows you to choose the type of font to use, make changes to the sizes of objects, assemble and organize designs, and more.

There are two sub-panels under the main panel. With the first sub-panel, you can give a name, save, and make cuts to your projects. The second panel gives you access to controls on the canvas area and editing functions.

Cricut Design Space Top Menu

A tap on this button brings out a whole list of other functions in the form of a menu. This Menu is quite handy. From here, you have access to your profile page and can make changes to your photo. The menu is not limited to this function, as there are other technical abilities it can provide, such as calibrating machine blades, updating your machine's software. Also, you can manage your Cricut Access account and subscription.

Uploading Images to Design Space

Images can be imported from other sources in different formats to the Design Space, where they can be converted to cuttable forms Go to Upload on the design panel at the left of the canvas area.

The Browse option opens the file selector to help you locate the particular image you want to work with. Apart from this option, you can use the drag and drop method to place the file into the upload section.

Different file formats go with different upload flows. For formats like .jpg, .png, .gif, .bmp, the Basic image upload flow is applied, while a selection of. svg or .dxf formats will require the Vector image upload flow.

Spacing of Letters

Designing takes different tactics and methods. One of them is moving letters together when making designs. This option, letter spacing, is applied to reduce space between letters, getting them together. To reduce the spaces, click on the down arrow. In some cases, letters may not be uniform; then, there's a need to, at first, ungroup the letters and move each until they overlap. A combination of the shift key and movement of the mouse will do the job. Hold the shift key down and move each letter using the mouse to make them remain on the same x-axis.

How to Weld, Slice, Flatten, Attach, Group/Ungroup, Delete/Duplicate, Color Sync.

The welding tool can easily combine two different shapes to form one whole shape.

To do this, create marks on the layer you want to weld.

Select Weld on the toolbar. The function will be affected.

The Slice tool is ideal for cutting off unnecessary shapes, letters, and other design elements in a project. To access this tool, there must be at least two layers at a time. The first object should be placed on the other, forming your preferred shape to cut out. Mark the formed object and then select Slice.

The Flatten option works in such a way that selected layers can be merged into a single layer. It is useful when you want to print your work. The Flatten tool is located at the right of the toolbar. You are to mark the layers of the design first before clicking Flatten.

Attach have some similarities with grouping option, but with more effect. Select all you want to remain in position for every piece of material, then click on Attach.

Designs can be quite complex, having many layers that sum its whole. The Group tool is useful for such designs. Grouping all layers keep it well organized. When moved around in the canvas area, all layers will be carried along, and nothing will be left off. The layers are first selected to use Group option, then the Group option.

Ungroup does the opposite of the Group option on

already selected layers on the canvas. The need to make some changes on the size, font type, or other elements of a layer or design might come up. Select the layer and click on the Ungroup tool located at the toolbar. You will see the effect immediately as the layers are separated.

The Duplicate option makes another copy of a selected layer or design on the canvas.

Delete removes elements already selected.

Color Sync is seen as the last option on the toolbar. The colors usually serve as a representation of different materials, in terms of colors. To use a particular color, drag that the color not required and drop it on the preferred color.

Getting Started with Text

To type text on the canvas area, go to the Text (T) icon on the left panel. A small window appears on the canvas. This is where the text is needed to be inputted. You are provided with various options for the text created, seen at the top of the screen. You can also edit text font, size, and style to suit your taste. In addition, changes can be made to the letter and line spacing.

How to Access Special Characters

Access to special characters comes with the Character Map, supported by Windows, or the Font Book, supported by Mac.

Go to the search panel on the computer system and type in "character map" to bring up the app. Launch it. A drop-down menu appears containing fonts that you can choose from, to work with. Go to the bottom. There is an option for Advanced View. Make sure you check the box. Make changes to the Character set by selecting Unicode and group by using Unicode Subrange. Another box will pop up for the Unicode Subrange. Go down the list, then select Private Use Characters. Select the special letters and make a choice. Click on Select after picking one, followed by Copy. Take off the letter you want to replace in the text box, then press Ctrl V on your keyboard to paste the special character.

How to Text Curve

The Curve tool functions by making bends on text to create circular shapes. In Design Space, this tool can be seen at the top of the canvas, specifically, the Text Edit space. When selecting the text, go straight to the Curve tool at the toolbar. A box having a slider appears immediately after the tool is clicked. Depending on a sphere diameter, a curve is given to the font or text nature.

With the left mouse button, drag to both right and left to make changes to the Diameter curvature of the text.

How to Make a Stencil?

The making of stencil starts with opening the file to be converted to a stencil. If your design is grouped, proceed with the next step; if not, all elements should be grouped.

- Move to the left-hand side of the canvas area—select shapes.
- The position of the square is taken to the right of the design. Select the Lock icon. This icon allows you to adjust the box to your preferred size.
- The design is then taken to the rectangle.
- Proceed to select the box and design made. Select Align, followed by Center. This process will center the design selected in horizontal and vertical manners.
- Still on selection mode, go to the Attach icon at the bottom of the screen to the right. For an easier route, right-click and select Attach.
- You can now cut the design. Select the Make It button at the top of the canvas area.

A Stencil is being made, and everything will come out in one color, so the design is seen on a mat. Place in the vinyl into the machine. Click on continue.

How to Use Contour with Text?

Making use of contour text comes first with welding (the text).

Have a go a selecting the text or word. Proceed with clicking on the button, Weld. This button is easily located at the bottom of the panel. The next step after welding is to contour the text. You also have a good go at taking off unwanted letters and removing blank spaces on a text which are quite unnecessary.

Vinyl for Cricut Projects

Vinyl is ideal for making sign works, decals, stencils, illustrations, and more. Two types of vinyl are very common; adhesive and heat transfer vinyl (HTV).

Adhesive Vinyl

This vinyl form creates a good combination with surfaces in which there's no need for heat to be applied. Adhesive vinyl is also divided into two types:

- Permanent adhesive is characteristic of its name; it permanently sticks to different surfaces and is not easily affected by any form of stress. It is generally great for works done outside.

- Removable adhesive: this type is good for indoor works. For example, wall decals. It is not permanent on surfaces as it easily comes off.

Heat Transfer Vinyl

Known simply as HTV or Iron-On Vinyl, this type has a great need for heat. The absence of heat makes it difficult to stick well to surfaces when applied.

There are numerous types of Heat Transfer Vinyl you can choose from. You also need iron and heat press to apply the vinyl to your work surface.

Vinyl Application Tips

Clean Your Surface

This act goes a long way in making your vinyl stay longer, and not only that, your design gets to stick in an ideal manner. Cleaning your surface comes easy. Just apply little alcohol on paper towel. Get to remove dust, dirt, oil, and debris accumulated over time due to not being in use for a long time or poor handling.

Applying Vinyl to a Rounded Surface

Rounded surface materials or objects are mugs or tumblers. The application of vinyl to these objects starts with making little sits on the transfer paper with scissors. Try not to make scouts on the weeded image.

Scraping on the Mat

Your design on the mat maintains its positioning. The scraper tool now comes in after unloading the cutting mat through the die-cutting machine. The tool is used to smoothen your project before the weeding process. The scraper should be used on the whole design, and make sure all layers and parts stick well to the mat.

You can Remove Your Vinyl Anytime

If the need arises to take off your vinyl from objects like mugs, apply heat from a heat gun, or make use of a blow dryer. At the stage where the vinyl is warm, take it off using the weeding tool by peeling from the surface. This method removes them easily without leaving out any residue.

Use the Right Kind of Vinyl

It is important you make use of vinyl with good quality as a poor one won't last for a long time, and also, the adhesive property won't be up to par. There's a high chance it can be damaged during weeding, meaning the material can't be used again, and you have to start the application all over. Whether the adhesive or heat transfer type, a good quality vinyl will provide you with some economic advantages.

Cricut Transfer Tape

This transfer tape is solely designed to make the process of transferring vinyl to your works, very easy. It has a clear film and grid to help you with the accurate positioning of your design. To apply a transfer tap:

- First, take the liner from the Transfer tape, off.
- Apply a part of the Transfer tape to either the center of the design or the end.
- Smoothen the Transfer Tape on the design using a Scraper tool. Start the process from within or center, outwards, where the Transfer tape was applied.
- Ensure you smoothen the back also.

Weeding Your Cricut Vinyl

The needed tools for the weeding process include the Cricut Weeding tool, True Control Knife, Pin Pen weeding tool, pair of scissors, and your Scraper tool.

The process centers on removing unwanted materials from the project. The Cricut Weeding tool has the look of a dental pick. It takes off tiny bits and parts of the vinyl design, such as the middle of the letter O. There's a high chance of damaging the vinyl if trying to remove these tiny parts without the Weeding tool.

Step by Step Cricut Projects to Get Started

Double-Sided Table Runner

You will need:

- Table Runner
- Smart Iron-On Vinyl
- Cricut Maker 3
- Cricut tools
- EasyPress

METHOD

- Spread the table runner on a flat surface. Measure out the area on the runner you'll be working with.

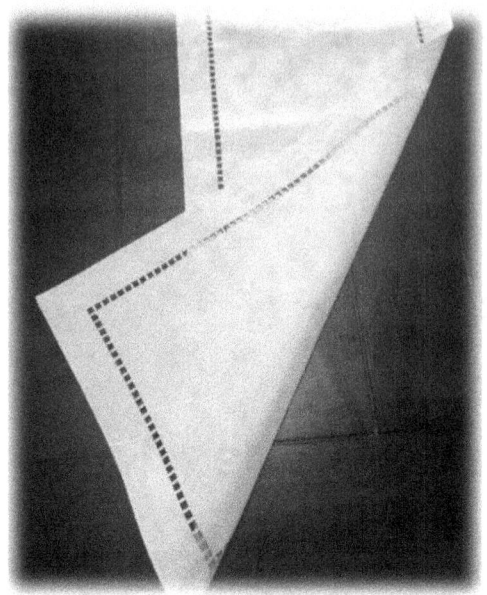

- With the Design Space, create shapes or any particular design you want to use. Ensure the measurements are same as that of the runner. Duplicate the design for both the front and back. For this work, a duplicated rectangle shape for both front and back is made with an inscription - Be Thankful.

- Prepare your ready Smart Iron-On vinyl. The length should be long enough to fit the whole design.

- The decision is yours to create another design for the other side. Search for images in the Design Space. Duplicate the image and contour both. Doing this allows each side to have its image. Take the measurements to make it fit into the shape used.

- Proceed to make it. A prompt is seen on display asking how you will load your materials to make the project. Select "Without Mat' since you're making use of Smart Iron-On Vinyl.

- You'll be shown an outlook of the work

coming out of the machine. You vet to mirror your images.

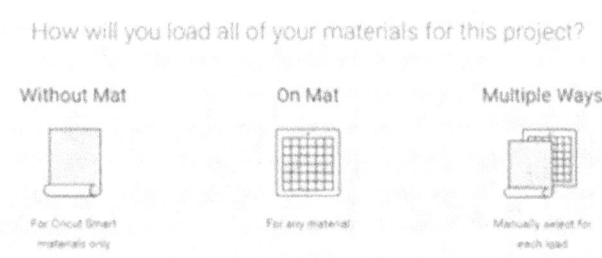

- Press Continue. The machine displays a response asking for a selection of the type of material. It allows you to select from the

available Smart Materials. Select Smart Iron-On.

- You'll see the Load button as it starts to blink. Get your vinyl, with the shiny side facing down. That shiny area is the Transfer sheet. You only want the machine to cut the vinyl. Place the vinyl underneath the rollers and press the Load button. The machine goes on to check if the material provided is enough. You'll notice the Go button flashing. Click it and watch the machine get to work.

- After cutting, remove the material from the machine. Cut out the unnecessary parts and Weed.

- Fold both the design and table runner in half. Use the creases to place the design on the center of the table runner.

- Press the design onto the table runner with EasyPress. The Cricut Heat guide provides information on the temperature and time.

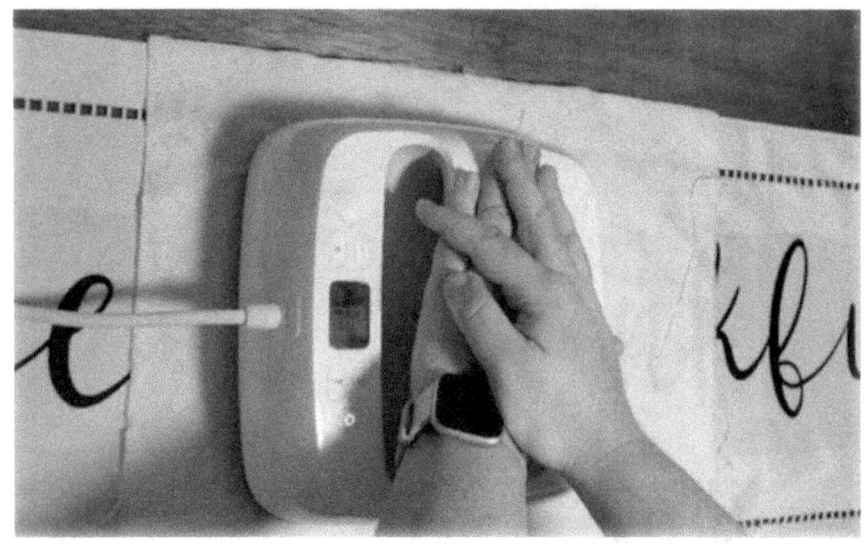

- Wait for it to cool, then take off the Transfer sheet.

- Apply this same process for the other side if using separate designs.

Simple Door Decal Project

You will need:

- Cricut Machine
- Cricut black vinyl
- Scraper tool
- Weeding tool
- Cricut Transfer tape

METHOD

- Make a pick of your preferred design quote. After this, go ahead to measure the door dimensions. The measurements must be in such a way that the design work fits into the panel perfectly.
- On your Design Space, input the quote to be used for the design.
- Type the design text on the canvas area. Do ensure that the words are well written in such a way that they

are easily read. You can set up a particular limit to the width, which can be adjusted to your taste after inputting the letters. Select a befitting font from the numerous fonts available to users.

> YOU DIDN'T COME THIS FAR TO ONLY COME THIS FAR.

- Make adjustments to the size of the quote. Move the whole work to a corner in the Design Space. Doing this prevents much vinyl from wasting, especially when making cuts. Well, this doesn't mean you should take it to the far ends or corners completely. You can give a little space of at least, 1/2".

- Proceed with the Design Space setup. There's a prompt to select the particular machine to sync with it automatically. Select the appropriate machine.

- After the design has been fully prepared, the next step is to cut. This is an effortless process by the machine itself. A preview is also provided to ensure it is just as you want.

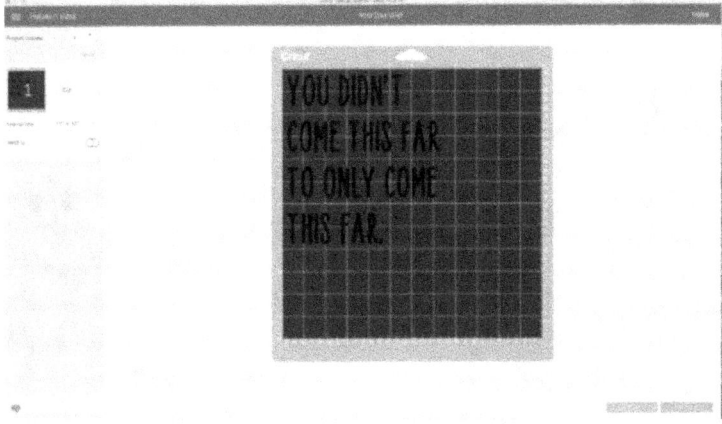

- Also, you are given the option to choose your material, making it as simple and smooth as it gets. Not too many thoughts are needed. The right kind of material determines the depth of cut made by the machine. For example, in a selected material like vinyl, the machine can make cuts through, but not going further than the backing.

- Once done with selecting the material in the Design Space, pick out the material, preferably black vinyl, and stick it to the mat. Use the Scraper tool to smoothen the surface, taking off air bubbles.

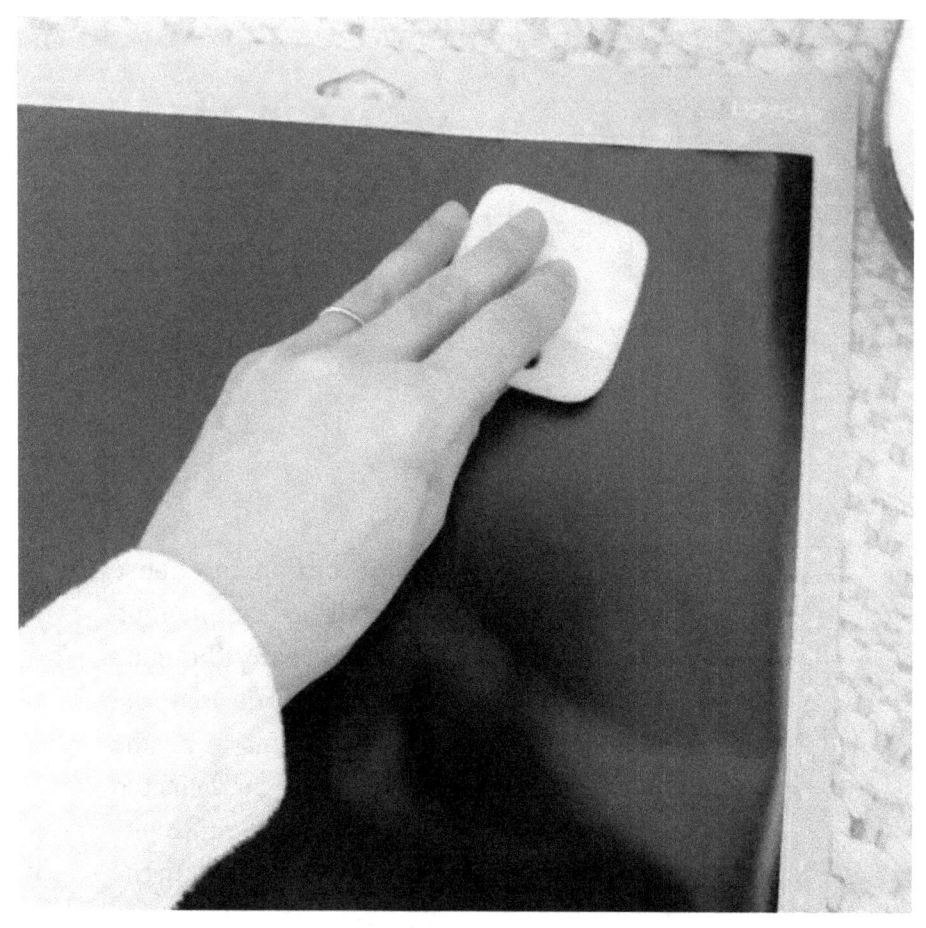

- The smoothening process prepares the material for proper loading into the machine.

- Fully ready for the next task, all that the Design Space requires from you is to press Go on the machine. It takes it up from there with efficient and precise quick cuts.

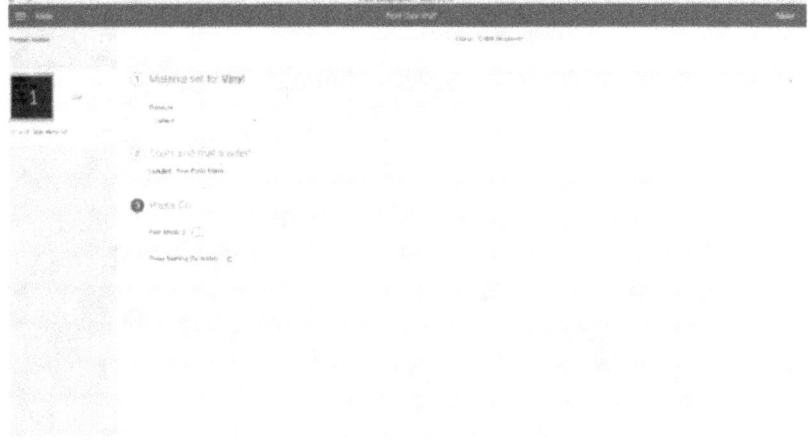

- Unload the material from the machine when cutting is over.

- The next is, preparation of the material (vinyl).
- Allow the backing of the material to remain when removing the cut material. The backing keeps the letters intact.

- Trim off unnecessary layers around the borders to reduce the size of the design. It makes it easier to work with that way.
- This is followed by removing the excess material not part of the design.

- Continue peeling off the material until

you're left with the letters alone.

- Some letters usually end up having some materials engraved within, for example, letters A and O. It depends on the wordings of the quote.

- In order to take out those materials inside the letters, if present, the Weeding tool is useful. This tool helps pull out engraved material.

- Get a transfer tape for the material used. Ensure the size is the same as that of the design. To do this, place the design on the transfer tape, mark the size on the tape, and cut out the shape.

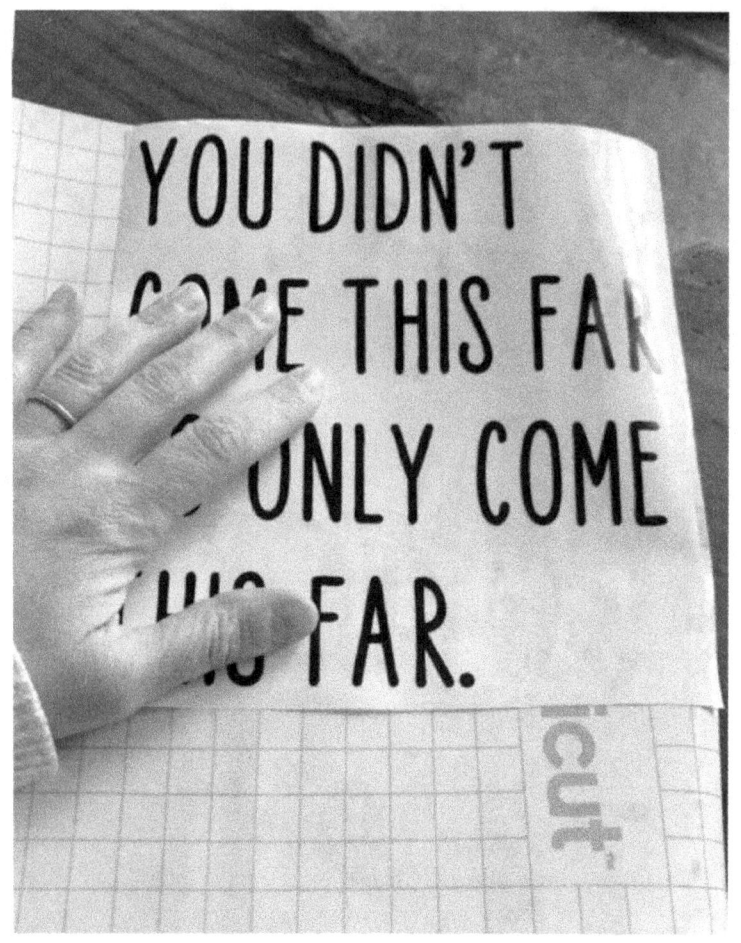

- After getting the size, remove the backing of the transfer tape; the tacky side. Place on the design front and press it down, starting from the corner.

- Air bubbles are seen, especially when pressing is done by hand. Use the Scraper tool to smoothen it further. This removes the air bubbles, ensuring a good adherence of transfer tape to the material used (vinyl).

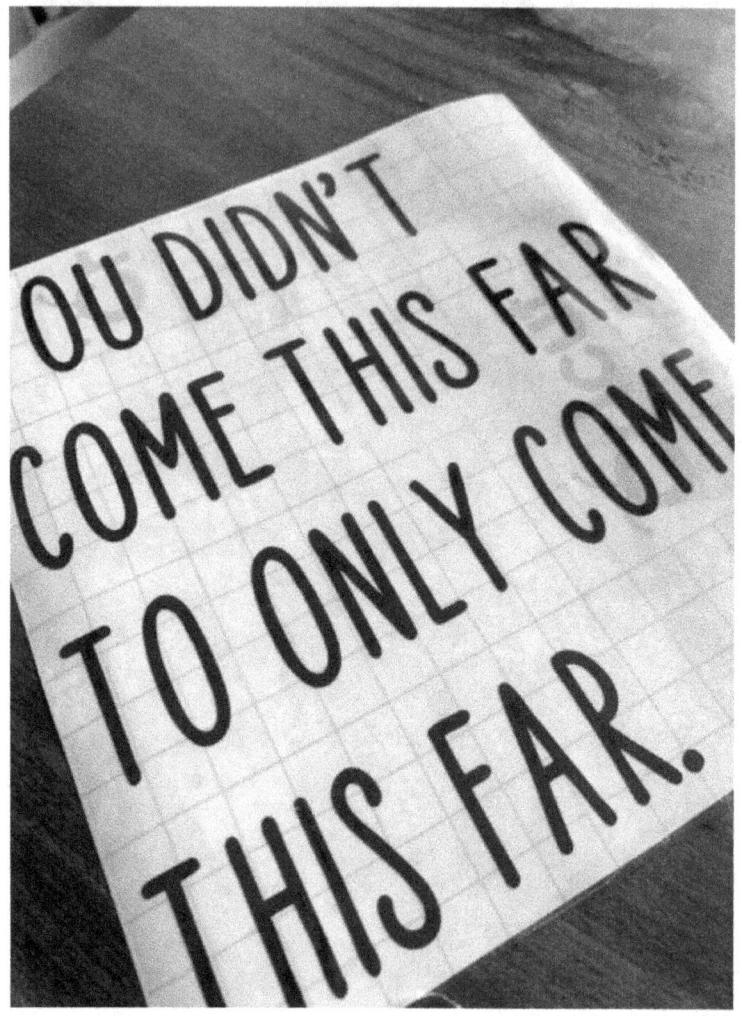

- The next step is placing your design on the door. Before this, make sure the door is quite clean and dry.

- Remove the material backing. Do this carefully to prevent ripping off any of the letters.

- You're now left with the transfer sheet and the already adhered lettering. Place the sheet on the door. Use the Scraper tool to press the material to the surface.
- Finally, take off the transfer sheet.

Pantry Labels

You will need:

- Black Cricut Permenate Vinyl
- Cricut Maker

- Cricut cutting mat – light grip
- Cricut Transfer Tape
- Cricut Tools

METHOD

- Select your desired font on the Design Space. Prepare it in a way you want it to appear on your project. The Design Space affords you the ability to make your designs.

- After preparing the font, take measurements of each container's front to note the size of each label. The next step is cutting.
- The Cricut machine is built to make the cutting process easy. It gives you a guide to making all the right settings for your work.

Just load the material used into the machine and press cut.

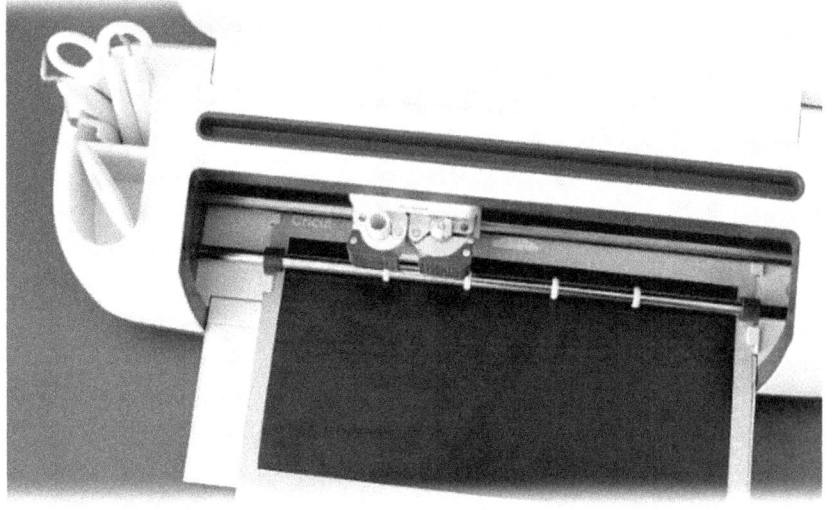

- After making the required cuts, apply the Weeding tool to take out unneeded material pieces.

- The Transfer tape comes in. The size should be such that it covers the label for your design. Place on the design and press it down to adhere firmly to the vinyl. Remove the Transfer tape.

- Adhere the tape having the labels on the container and press down firmly to ensure the vinyl is in position. Remove the Transfer tape finally.

Custom Pillowcase

You will need:

- Cricut Smart Iron-On, Black
- Cricut Maker 3
- Weeder Tool
- EasyPress 9x9
- Pillowcase
- EasyPress Mat
- Heat Resistant Tape
- Lint Roller

METHOD

- The first step is creating your design. In creating this particular design for this project, add text to the canvas area, and input the names you want to use. Get the measurement of your pillow size and create a square of the same size. The square serves as a template to size the names. Delete square after getting the required size of text.

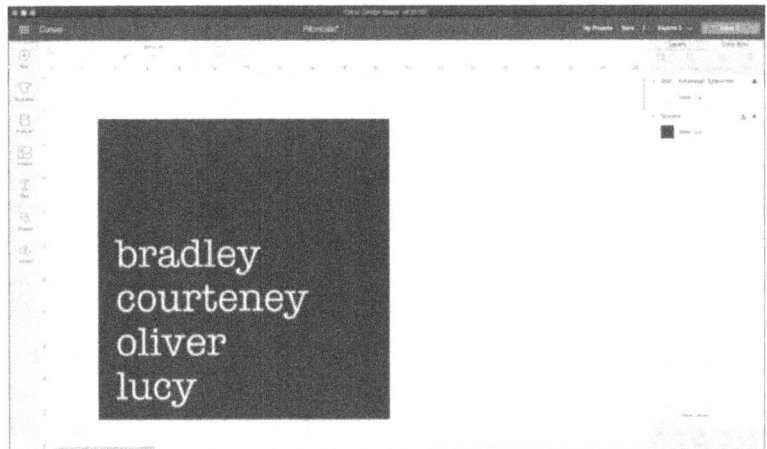

- Click on the Make It button, and you're prompted on loading options. Select Without Mat, followed by Done.

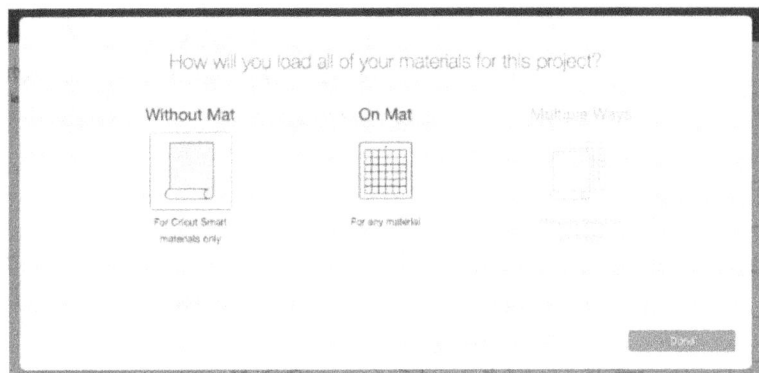

- Go to Mirror. This is seen on the left side of the screen. Click the button underneath. The button turns green on selection. Select Continue, and then, Smart Iron-On, for your cutting setting.

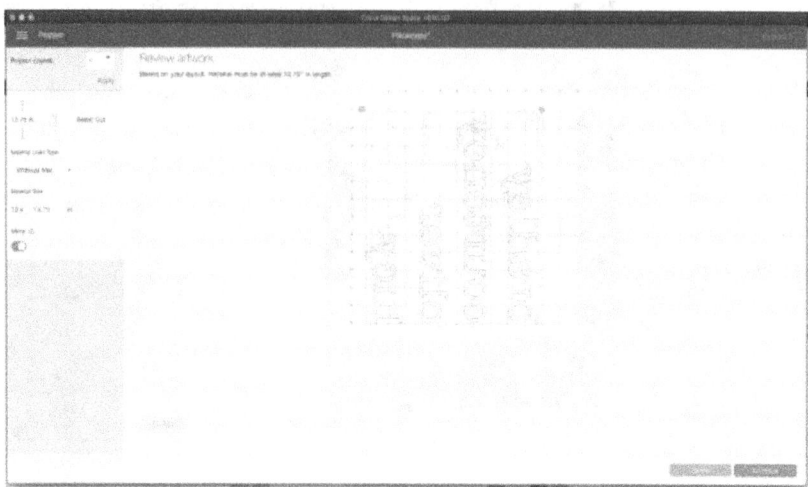

- The next step is loading your Smart Iron-On into the machine. Make sure the shiny side is facing down. On insertion, slide the material along the left guide under the white. Apply pressure up against the roller. The

Load/Unload button flashes as this process is completed. Press the button, and the machine pulls in the material. Press the Go button when the machine is ready to cut. Unload when done.

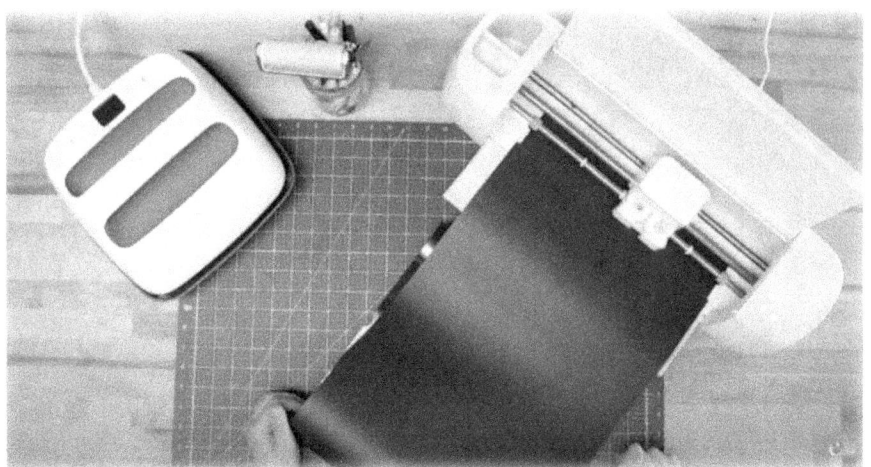

- Remove unwanted Iron-on from the design with the Weeding tool. Note that vinyl is removed from the dull/matte side. Do well not to damage the Transfer sheet.

- The design is transferred to the pillowcase with the Transfer sheet and EasyPress. The EasyPress should be set to a temperature of 315F and within the time of 30 seconds. Allow it to heat up. During heating up, the EasyPress mat is placed inside the pillowcase. In the absence of a mat, use a towel. Ensure the whole area to be worked on is covered.

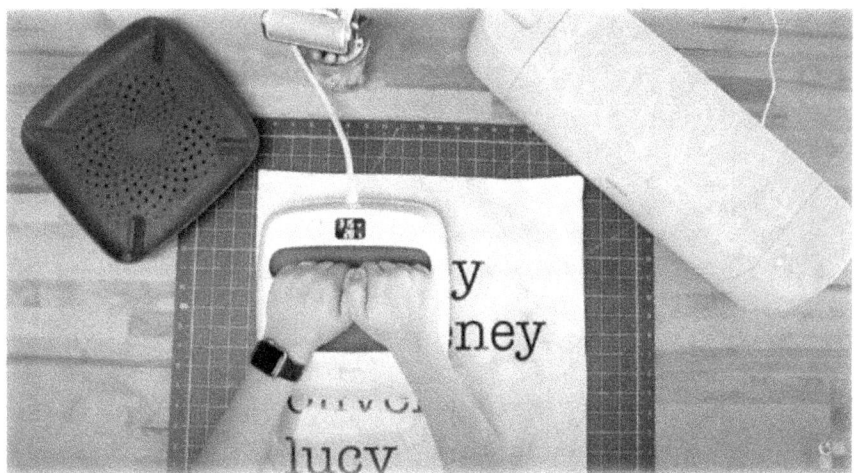

- Preheat the pillowcase for a few seconds and apply the design. Use heat-resistant tape to hold it in position. Use the EasyPress on the pillowcase for 30 seconds. Do same for the back. Allow it to cool, then take off the liner.

FREQUENTLY ASKED QUESTIONS on Cricut maker 3

Here are some frequently asked questions about the

Cricut Maker 3.

Did the Maker 3 Drop Some Functions from Previously Existing Machines?

It didn't. It performs the same functions as the other machines, especially the Cricut Maker, and even more. It can make prints and cuts. Also, you can make drawings, score, engrave and make use of mats. There is a great improvement to speed, power, and new matless cutting technology, all for a great crafting experience for users.

Do the Current Maker Tools Function with Maker 3?

Yes. Tools such as pens, blades, mats, and others, function well with the Cricut Maker 3.

How Large Can I Cut on the Cricut Maker 3?

The size you can cut is 144" in length using Smart Vinyl and 48" from a Smart Iron-On material for a single image. But with a roll of 21", you can cut three quantities of 84" images or that of 120" at once.

Are Mats Still Needed for Maker 3?

Yes. You still need mats, and they can work with the Maker 3. Not all materials are Smart. Materials like fabric, chipboard, leather, felt, matboard, and others need mat to work. Likewise, mats are handy for vinyl, iron-on, and paper.

Can Smart Materials Be Used with Cricut Maker?

Not at all. You can only use Smart Materials on Cricut

Maker 3 and Explore 3. They have been designed with sensors and guides to load and control the materials. The previous Cricut versions don't have sensors and can't work on Smart Materials or matless cutting.

Conclusion

We've come to the end of our journey among the best cricut project ideas! You've got this!

If someone asks you, "why Cricut?" you can answer with confidence that it allows you to get more done in less time and gives you the perfect platform to make all your creative ideas a reality. You're not limited by tools or materials, because your machine can handle almost anything you want to try.

By the way, if you're ever confronted by a "I-do-everything-by-hand" crafter who questions your prowess, simply ask her to create something using your Cricut and then wait for the excuses as to why she can't "right now."

I need to point this out because too many new crafters and artists get discouraged when they come across people who insist "real crafting" is done by hand.

They plant seeds of doubt and, before you know it, you've given up on your hobby or craft. Never forget that being able to use Cricut's design software, operating a Cricut machine, and making the final product takes a lot of skill, imagination, and creativity—and you've got them all. While it is relatively easy to learn how to use a Cricut machine, it's certainly difficult (grueling, even) to use it without knowledge and training. If it weren't, there would be no need for Cricut books, blogs, and social media groups. (And, of course, new Cricut machines wouldn't spend weeks or months tucked away in closets.)

When it comes to operating a Cricut machine, you now know it involves basic steps, regardless of the model you own. It always starts with finalizing your design on Design Space and culminates when you press that Go button. Further, you learned about each Cricut machine's features. In fact, you know enough about their differences to guide anyone you know to choose the best model. You can even help another crafter set up their new machine. Hey, Cricut is contagious, so you'll soon have your own Cricut Newbie to guide!

On a final note, I would like to thank you for giving yourself the opportunity to dive into the exciting world of Cricut crafting.

Think of this book as your personal Cricut companion, always ready to give a hand if something slips your mind. Keep it close and share what you learn with other Cricut beginners.

Above all, let it be a constant reminder of how much you deserve to have a ton of fun.

Happy crafting!

www.ingramcontent.com/pod-product-compliance
Lightning Source LLC
Chambersburg PA
CBHW050249120526
44590CB00016B/2280